UNDER THE SUN

DESERT STYLE AND ARCHITECTURE

TEXT BY

SUZI MOORE

PHOTOGRAPHS BY

TERRENCE MOORE

FOREWORD BY

STEWART L. UDALL

A BULFINCH PRESS BOOK

LITTLE, BROWN AND COMPANY

BOSTON • NEW YORK • LONDON

First paperback edition, 1999

First hardcover edition, 1995
Second printing, 1999

LIBRARY OF CONGRESS CATALOGING-IN-PUBLICATION DATA

Moore, Suzi.
Under the sun : desert style and architecture / text by Suzi Moore ; photographs by
Terrence Moore ; foreword by Stewart L. Udall. — 1st ed.
p. cm.
"A Bulfinch Press book."
Includes bibliographic references.
ISBN 0-8212-2226-0 (hc)   ISBN 0-8212-2587-1 (pb)
1. Architecture, Domestic — Arid regions. 2. Interior decoration — Human factors.
I. Moore, Terrence. II. Title.
NA7117.A74M66 1995
728'.0915'4 — dc20   95-11432

Photographs on page 47 (right) and page 144 (top) are copyright © by Suzi Moore.

Page 1:   Sunrise in Alamos, Sonora, illuminates the bell tower of the cathedral.
Page 2:   The red tile roofs and whitewashed stone walls of this Andalusian hilltown are typical of
            southern Spain.
Page 3:   The blue door and stone wall are characteristic of the many mosques on the island of
            Djerba, Tunisia.
Pages 6–7: Beyond the last village of M'Hamid, in Morocco, on the southeast side of the Atlas
            Mountains, is the erg, or the vast sea of sand of the Sahara.

BULFINCH PRESS IS AN IMPRINT AND TRADEMARK OF LITTLE, BROWN AND COMPANY (INC.)

DESIGNED BY PAUL ZAKRIS AND JEANNE ABBOUD

PRINTED IN JAPAN

A VERY SPECIAL THANK YOU TO:

My father, the late great Sam Sneller, for all the wonderful hikes in the desert and his many words of wisdom.
My mother, Fran Sneller, for her endless words of encouragement.
Brady and Morgan Barnes, two wonderful children who make life more interesting.

—SUZI MOORE

My parents, Lois and Leeland Tenney, and my teacher Darrell McOmber
for their help with my seventh-grade science project, making my very first adobe bricks.

—TERRENCE MOORE

ACKNOWLEDGMENTS

We would also like to thank all of those who gave their time and knowledge to help make this book a reality, including Jeanne Abboud, Bernie and Trish Abramson, Ernesto Baell, Bruce Barnard, Keith Behner, Alice Billings, Jean-Louis Bourgeois and Carollee Pelos, Richard Brittain, Ben Brown, Janet Burner, Barney Burns and Mahina Drees, Mark Butler, Scott and Cindy Cameron, Linda Campbell, Norman Carver, Madelaine Cassidy, Raima Chalmers, Yvon Chouinard, Kenneth Clark, Ed Crocker, Bill and Debbie Davis, Jennifer Doherty, Dawna Ferris, Gillispie County Historical Society, Inc., Dr. Joe S. Graham, Gary and Deborah Holley, Bud and Barbara Hoover, Nader Khalili, Jeff Litton, Dr. Charles Lowe, Judy and Michael Margolis, Paul Martin, Joe Martinez, Mike and Happy Matthews, Paul McHenry, Sally McManus, Lynn Meyers, Matts Myrhman, Native Seeds Search, Charles and Peggy Nugent, Janice O'Leary, Palm Springs Historical Society, Richard Patenaude, Tom Pew, Lynn Pirozoli, Mary Powers, Rancho Santa Fe Association, Bob Rea, Chiara Amarosa Roll, San Antonio Conservation Society, Rick Schlesinger, Jane Sievert, Linette Shorr, Ed Smart, Ron and Marsha Spark, Larry Speck, Paige Springer, Jim Stanfield, Irmine Steltzner, Texas Historical Commission, Tourist Office of Spain, Los Angeles, Skip Wells, Sharon Wickson, Paul Zakris.

Also our appreciation to the following sponsors: Eagle Creek Travel Gear, Iberia Airlines, Kodalux, Patagonia Clothing Company, Pentax Corporation, Sierra Designs.

And, finally, our special thanks to our two editors: Jennie Bernard, without whose help this project would still be a dream; and Janet Bush, the project's savior and our esteemed editor.

CONTENTS

FOREWORD

Ten thousand years ago, long before the Great Pyramid was constructed, humans were living in the desert. These first desert dwellers were nomads, herders who roamed the trackless realms, sleeping under the stars or in simple tents. With the advent of agriculture, portable shelters evolved into permanent ones. Desert architecture was born.

Who designed and constructed the first desert houses is unknown. But it would not have taken long for these first builders to discover that thick earthen walls could buffer the summer heat, and that a building could be cunningly constructed to provide shade and collect cooling breezes, as well as warmth from the winter sun. The first walls to rise from the desert floor were as distinctive in appearance as the landscape into which they blended. Like an igloo on sea ice, they possessed the intrinsic *rightness* that is the hallmark of enduring design — and the motif of this book.

More than two years ago, Suzi and Terrence Moore embarked on an odyssey that would carry them halfway around the globe. Their aim was to capture in words and pictures that elusive essence of form married to function that characterizes timeless design. By temperament and experience, the two were uniquely qualified to succeed on their quest. Both have a firm grasp of the desert's architectural history and a discerning eye for the sensual details that give it its charm. Of equal importance, they have an understanding of, and appreciation for, deserts themselves. They know where the boojum tree grows, the smell of desert rain, the sound of quail at dawn. Like the buildings they depict, they are natives. Their book is an eloquent celebration of what might be called desert style. It will appeal to architects and builders, to students of design, to anyone who has ever lived in the desert or dreamed of doing so.

Much of this book's value derives from its expansive focus, its depth of field. The Moores did not confine their search just to this country. They scoured the Southwest — but they also flew east across the Atlantic to photograph in North Africa, jeeped south to survey Mexico, and tracked back down the centuries to celebrate the building accomplishments of the vanished Anasazi. Of these disparate pieces, they have made a whole. They tie the Kasbahs of Morocco to the Indian pueblos of New Mexico, and the ancient cliff dwellings of Mesa Verde to the futuristic structures built of recycled tires known as Earthships. The book is full of echoes: The mud-and-straw plaster in Tunisia is reminiscent of Taos. A mosque in Morocco suggests a mission in Mexico. As for construction materials, there is more than adobe here: a limestone ranch house in Texas and a straw-bale structure outside Santa Fe share space with a wattle-and-daub home in Mexico and a frame stucco mansion in California. Shelter is more than a roof overhead, the Moores seem to believe, and good design is a form of wealth available to rich and poor alike.

Although its focus is desert architecture,

this book serves to remind us of a deeper truth that has been obscured in recent decades, as cheap energy and air-conditioning have spawned a sprawl of buildings that, to my eye, appear as transient as tumbleweeds. That truth is this: The most important building "covenants" are those dictated by the earth. If a dwelling fails to heed its surroundings, if it is not energy and resource efficient, if it does not make frugal and elegant use of local building materials, then it cannot, will not, ever be beautiful. At a time when much contemporary architecture appears, on closer inspection, to be mere artifice, *Under the Sun* demonstrates that the designs that endure are the organic ones, those that are rooted in place.

If we moderns, who on average spend 80 percent of our time indoors, wish to exist in harmony with our environment, we must do by choice what the ancients did by necessity — design with the earth and climate in mind. After all, in the long run, our dwellings shape us more than we shape them. For anyone who seeks to comprehend that special wisdom of the desert, this book is a splendid trailhead.

— Stewart L. Udall
Santa Fe, New Mexico

INTRODUCTION

The desert is a land filled with surrealistic flat-topped mesas and teetering spires, long vistas and shifting sands, badlands and lava fields, occasionally broken up by small pockets of green oases. It is a place of deep silences marked by torrential summer rains or extreme aridness, with long cycles of drought and dust-laden air. When evening approaches, desert colors begin to change from a brilliant white light to a sulfuric yellow, then crimson and deep purple.

Overall, deserts are dry, although the amount of rainfall and humidity can vary widely in any given year. Deserts can be high, such as that on the south side of the Atlas Mountains in Morocco, with its snow-dusted peaks and frigid winds that whip around hillsides or its intense heat that settles into the valleys. The high sagebrush country of northern New Mexico and Arizona is characterized by dramatic extremes of chilling white winters and sun-blinding summers. Deserts can be low, like the Anza-Borrego Desert in California, which at one point sinks to 273 feet below sea level. The long summers are unbearably hot, while brief winters remain mild. There are coastal deserts, which include most of the shoreline around Baja California, a place of both cold winds and early morning fog, which dissipates quickly with the heat of the day, or of warm breezes and burning heat. In the desert it is possible to have temperature extremes of fifty degrees in a twenty-four-hour period. The lack of humidity allows the sun to heat the earth quickly, but the dry air releases the heat during the night.

Desert architecture must take into consideration extremes of temperature, aridity, and availability of water. For people to live comfortably in any desert location, certain design elements must be carefully addressed, including building materials, site orientation, and the spatial flow of the house.

Building materials used for desert structures play an important role in keeping interior temperatures stable. As the earliest man discovered, indigenous materials such as stone, earth, and native woods can be developed into well-insulated spaces. In parts of Morocco, Tunisia, southern Spain, and Texas, limestone is a common geological element used extensively for floors and walls. Vaults, domes, and arches are constructed out of limestone blocks in Tunisia, a region with little usable timber other than palm wood. The mesas of northern Arizona and New Mexico, and southern Colorado and Utah, provide an abundance of native sandstone, used for building houses as well as contemporary Indian pueblos. Sandstone was also used by ancient Indians in the construction of large multistoried pueblos.

Another common building material is adobe, a word taken from the Arabic language, referring to bricks made from unbaked earth. An additive of straw helps conduct moisture from the center of the adobe block, preventing cracking. This age-old technique can be found around the world. In Morocco, Spain, Mexico, and the Southwest of the United States, wood forms are still turning out adobe bricks that will be used in desert dwellings. Spain introduced the adobe brick to the New World at a time when pueblos were built with coursed adobe, a method of building walls with a stiff mixture of mud heaped on course after course, and with wattle and daub, a type of construction using a mud mixture to fill and plaster a woven skeletal frame made from reeds and branches. Pisé, or rammed earth, is another form of earth construction used extensively throughout the desert world. Moist earth, sometimes mixed with straw, is tamped into wall forms, then allowed to cure before adding the next level.

Because of population shifts and environmental problems, there are great demands on the resources of the contemporary American Southwest. In response, there is a reemergence of vernacular architecture as well as an exploration of alternative housing. Waste products are becoming treasured building materials, producing structures such as the Earthships in Taos, New Mexico, where old tires and aluminum cans are used to construct massive walls. A house outside Santa Fe is built with bales of straw, an agricultural by-product that is easy to stack and has a high insulation rating. Adobe brickmaking is now a science. Soils are carefully analyzed, then mixed with additives, such as asphalt emulsion and cement, that make them impervious to moisture. A contemporary home in the California desert uses glass walls that roll back into structural walls, turning rooms into ramadas, or freestanding porches that open to the breezes. Solar power has been harnessed, providing energy to run refrigerators, lights, toilets, and hot-water heaters.

As our predecessors understood, orientation is also essential to living in harmony with our climate and landscape. Using a method similar to that of burrowing animals, the people of Matmata, Tunisia, build barriers, living in rooms dug far below the surface of the earth around an open crater or pit. In the troglodyte (cave) communities of North Africa and southern Spain, houses are hollowed out of the hillsides, providing insulation against the intense summer sun.

The hilltop residents of Montefrio, Spain, and the ancient Anasazi of the Southwest built shelters under overhangs that created a shield from the blast of summer heat, while exposing themselves to solar gain in cooler weather. A recently built house in Santa Fe is based on some of these same principles, bermed into a southern slope away from the cold winter winds of the high desert, while exposed to the low sun on the open sides. In places that are not bermable, walls can create shade, such as the walls at the Kasbah of Aït Benhaddou in Morocco. The high, close-together walls block the sun most of the day, and their mass of adobe provides insulation, a result which is not unlike that achieved by the pueblo dwellings of the Southwest. The long, blank northern walls of the Acoma pueblo in New Mexico protect the apartment-style complexes from the cold northern winds, and the stepped-back terraces on the south extend the living area to the outside. Many towns in Mexico and Spain use *portales*, or porches, and *zaguanes*, or covered breezeways, to shade walls and provide outside covered living spaces. Interior courtyards, common in Spain and northern Mexico, offer light, air, and a sanctuary from the outside world.

Crucial to all desert life is water. Civilizations have managed to thrive in arid environments, locating valuable water sources and turning brown into green by damming and diverting water, capturing runoff, and sinking deep wells. The earliest-known dam was built on the Nile River by the Egyptians in 2800 B.C. The ancient Iranians transported water in underground tunnels. The Hohokam Indians of the Southwest, also known as the Canal Builders, built miles of open irrigation canals around Phoenix. Centuries later, Jack Swilling, a prospector, noticed the canals and began developing the region as an agricultural community. There are Berbers in Tunisia and Hopi Indians in northern Arizona who practice dry farming, often terracing slopes in order to capture runoff, a method similar to that used by Michael Reynolds in Taos. In his designs, cisterns with filtering systems collect and store water for household use. Another idea rooted in centuries of desert living is a pool of water oriented in the direction of the prevailing breezes, functioning as an outdoor evaporative cooler. An enclosed courtyard in northern Mexico utilizes a small pond to capture breezes that sweep through the openings. A cliff house in Baja California opens up to the ocean, taking advantage of the cool winds that blow across the water. In Texas, a ranch house with a screened living area faces a large pond that cools down the hot air. Wells tapped into groundwater sources, whether hand dug or drilled, provide water for much of the arid world. Pipelines also carry water hundreds of miles, allowing large urban areas that have no water supply of their own to exist.

Parallel with man are the botanical survivors, or desert plants, with their specialized adaptations for living in inhospitable landscapes. Root systems plunge downward, tapping into deep water reserves, similar to drilling a well, or spread horizontally, close to the surface, capturing runoff from infrequent rainstorms, like the dry farmers of the world. There are drought evaders, or desert annuals, that endure drought as dormant seeds. Drought avoiders include cacti and other succulents. They have a thick waxy cuticle that holds water inside and stomata, or small pores, that open at night to avoid water loss — like shutters on windows, closed during the hot summer days and opened to the cool nighttime air. Water spenders seek out riparian habitats and have extensive root systems with taproots that can reach groundwater as deep as 150 feet below the earth's surface. The drought-tolerant plants survive by exposing less surface area to the air with smaller leaves that can be shed during times of drought. These are plants that can play an integral role in desert

architecture, one that need not deplete precious water reserves. Trees, such as the mesquite and paloverde, can be planted in strategic locations in order to provide shade. Ground covers hold on to precious soils, defeating the erosional effects of summer rains. Exterior wall coverings of shrubs and vines minimize the amount of surface area directly exposed to the sun. For example, the Mennonites of Chihuahua, Mexico, use large deciduous trees and vines to shade the walls of their homes during the summer months.

Over the past several decades, many of the age-old concepts essential for living in the desert have been ignored, resulting in serious problems, such as depletion of groundwater and fossil fuels, erosion caused by poor land management, and the creation of heat sinks made from concrete and pavement, which increase the surface temperature of the earth. By considering the historic roots of desert design, today's architecture can and must learn from the past without being bound by tradition. The following pages present both ancient dwellings and contemporary houses that deal successfully with the difficulties of desert living in such regions as Tunisia, Morocco, southern Spain, northern Mexico, and the greater Southwest — regions connected by climate, landscape, and architecture.

TUNISIA AND MOROCCO

The Sahara, or Sahra, meaning "desert" in Arabic, is the largest expanse of desert in the world, covering roughly three and a half million square miles of land surface in North Africa, an area equivalent in size to the United States. It has a fragile ecosystem, characterized by extremes. Elevations range from one hundred feet below sea level to more than 11,500 feet. Temperatures can soar to 135 degrees Fahrenheit during summer days, with a ground temperature of 170 degrees Fahrenheit, then plummet more than 50 degrees as

night takes over, the humidity rarely exceeding 10 percent. For most of the year the skies take on a harsh, often unbearable blinding light; the intense heat can dehydrate a person without water in one day. Sculpted sand dunes, windswept and moving, are constantly encroaching on and claiming new territory. In spite of this, only 20 percent of the Sahara has been swallowed up by sand. The rest is covered by either vast stretches of dry rock-strewn plains or chains of mountains and plateaus that zigzag across a land scarred with deep canyons carved by infrequent rainstorms. In this desert region, where a small spring produces an oasis, many past civilizations created unique ways of life in order to survive. Man, like the animals and plants of the desert, has successfully adapted to living in this climatic inferno.

TUNISIA

Tunisia occupies only a small section of the vast Sahara. Flanked by the Mediterranean Sea on the north and east coasts, and Algeria to the west, the country has a varied terrain. The Atlas Mountains form a rain shadow, blocking moisture from reaching the southern side of the slopes, while a lush agricultural belt thrives in the northern coastal region, known as the Tell. The Mejerda River, the only one in Tunisia that has year-round water, crosses through the Tell, helping to support a large population. The central area, known as the Steppe, has both high and low elevations with very little vegetation due to poor soils and unpredictable rainfall. In the south, the land rises up to form plateaus and barren hills. Large salt-filled depressions, or chotts, glisten for miles with white shiny crystals that create mirages, shimmering illusions of water. Between these inhospitable landforms are a few scattered oases.

Each of the villages in Tunisia has a special way of adapting to the landscape and climate. A great deal of resourcefulness and ingenuity is required to live in a land as hot, arid, and empty as the Sahara. The Tunisians solve the problem of roofing with no available wood by using vaults and domes created from limestone blocks. They use the thickness of limestone and earthen walls built into south-facing hillsides, or carve out troglodyte communities, to produce stable interior temperatures. And by staggering the heights of their gardens to

ABOVE: TYPICAL CONSTRUCTION ON THE ISLAND OF DJERBA, TUNISIA, USES LIMESTONE BLOCKS TO FORM ARCHES, DOMES, AND VAULTS. WOOD, OTHER THAN PALM, IS SCARCE. INTERIOR AND EXTERIOR WALLS ARE PLASTERED AND WHITEWASHED, CREATING REFLECTIVE SURFACES.

BELOW: TUNNELED PASSAGEWAYS WITH THICK ADOBE WALLS AND BUILT-IN MASONRY BENCHES PROVIDE A RETREAT FROM THE MIDDAY SUN AT THE KASBAH GLAOUI TAOURIRT OUTSIDE OUARZAZATE, MOROCCO.

create shade, along with employing terracing and irrigation, they have made productive agriculture a reality. Their vital and creative approach to living in a harsh desert environment has inspired organic styles of architecture that not only meet basic needs but also celebrate forms and shapes that reflect and merge with the natural landscape.

MOROCCO

The strong winds of the Moroccan Sahara blow fine particles of sand across the land, shaping them into piles that continuously shift and change. The winds move over plains and mountains, swirling and spinning into narrow passes, finding their way around the various ranges, and out again across the plateaus.

Morocco boasts one of the most multidimensional landscapes and climates in North Africa. Split into sections by a string of mountains and plateaus, and then severed again by hills, plains, and sandy wastelands, the country is bound by the Atlantic to the west and the Mediterranean to the north— approximately eleven hundred miles of coastline. The northern inland coastal plain is dominated by rich agricultural fields and represents most of the country's wealth and population. The mountainous midsection acts as a barrier to moisture-laden clouds. These mountains ultimately fold back down into the southern valleys, rocky plains, and vast stretches of sand that are dissected by four main river courses, three of which vanish into the Saharan sands.

Villages balance on the edge of cliffs or are clustered beside watercourses that channel down from the snowcapped Atlas into the valleys below. With villages located against a protective hillside, and compounds enclosed with high blank walls, communities are effectively insulated from the cold winds that come down out of the mountains and are protected from the blowing sand of the desert. On the rocky slopes of the mountains, houses are constructed with limestone; in the lower regions they are made with brown clay bricks and pisé, or rammed earth — earth rammed into wood forms. Doorways are recessed and shaded; windows are high and small, with roof terraces that provide extended living spaces.

CHENINI

LEFT: THE ANCIENT *KSAR* IN THE BERBER VILLAGE OF CHENINI IS FORMED OF LIMESTONE BLOCKS FROM THE HILLSIDE. THE COMPLEX FOLLOWS THE CONTOUR OF THE MOUNTAIN, SPIRALING UP TO THE TOP OF THE RIDGE.

RIGHT: DOORS IN CHENINI ARE MADE FROM SPLIT PALM TRUNKS, THE ONLY AVAILABLE WOOD IN THE AREA.

The village of Chenini in southern Tunisia is camouflaged by a rough desert landscape covered with small mountains of sharp rocks, long valleys of desert pavement, and little vegetation to distract the eye. Perched on a hillside ledge, the village overlooks a narrow valley where natural drainageways cut through the sides of adjoining slopes. Low walls made from rubble partition each drainage into terraces that trap enough water to grow date palms and support a few small gardens. Houses are either built from the local limestone or excavated directly into the hillside following the natural topography of the land. Walled yards create outdoor living areas for washing and cooking. The facades are flattened out, covered with plaster, and have holes cut through them for doors made from split palm. Window openings are small, allowing only a minimal amount of light. Nearby, animal enclosures built from rubble and palm trunks house burros, sheep, camels, and chickens. Blue-eyed Berber women, displaying tattooed faces, hands, and feet, haul water, a treasured commodity, from a well below the village in large plastic containers loaded on burros.

The ruins of an old *ksar* lie on an adjacent hillside beyond the populated area. The *ksar*, originally built as a fort for protection against invading Arabs, was later used for storage and is now occupied by only a handful of people and animals. The *ksar*, built of limestone blocks stacked high to form walls, mimics the landscape. These apartment-style buildings grow out from the crest of the ridge, following the spine of the hillside and fitting unobtrusively into the landscape. Doorways have odd shapes: some are uneven rectangles; others have an arch at the top. The individual units, or *ghorfas*, are stacked on top of each other several stories high. Paths spiral around the hill leading from one level to the next.

Not far from the village a scree-laden track ascends to a small mosque cradled between two stony hills. Breezes blow through the pass while clouds build up to the south, but the moisture evaporates before it ever reaches the ground. The minaret, or tower of the mosque, leaning to one side, looks like a rocket ready to be launched. In contrast, the roofline emerges from the hillside as a

TOP: IN CHENINI, LOCALS FILL THEIR BARRELS WITH WATER FROM THE WELL AND THEN HAUL THEM UP THE HILL TO THEIR HOMES. THE WELL IS THE ONLY NEARBY SOURCE OF WATER FOR DRINKING, WASHING, AND WATERING THEIR ANIMALS.

BOTTOM: INSIDE ONE OF THE *GHORFAS*, OR STORAGE ROOMS, OF THE OLD *KSAR* IN CHENINI IS A LARGE URN USED FOR GRAIN OR WATER.

TOP: BETWEEN THE OLD *KSAR* AND THE NEW VILLAGE AT CHENINI IS A WHITE MOSQUE WITH ITS MINARET, THE FOCAL POINT OF MOST COMMUNITIES IN NORTH AFRICA.

BOTTOM: A MOSQUE IS CRADLED BETWEEN TWO HILLS OUTSIDE THE VILLAGE OF CHENINI. THE ROOF IS MADE UP OF A SERIES OF DOMES, SHAPES THAT MIRROR THE LANDSCAPE.

In the village of Chenini man-made forms emulate the landscape through the use of native materials. The dwellings serve as practical housing in a remote area with little access to materials from the outside world.

series of domes. Arched windows and doors echo the shape of the dome, eliminating the need for alternative, but scarce, building materials such as wood. Around the perimeter are low rock walls, carefully fitted together without mortar. The thick native limestone used for the mosque ensures stable interior temperatures.

MATMATA

LEFT: IN MATMATA, TUNISIA, MAN-MADE CRATERS CREATE A COURTYARD FOR THE SUBTERRANEAN ROOMS DUG OUT AROUND THE PERIMETER.

RIGHT: A MASONRY STAIRWAY ON AN OUTSIDE EARTHEN WALL LEADS TO THE SECOND FLOOR OF A CRATER HOME IN MATMATA. TUNNELS OR RAMPS SERVE AS ENTRANCES TO THE MAN-MADE CRATERS.

In this part of south-central Tunisia, the land looks like a place of despair, desolate and forgotten. Soft textureless hills run all the way to the horizon and vanish in a cloud of dust. An oppressive heat seems never to let up. When a strong wind blows, fine particles of stinging sand make seeing difficult. In this inhospitable and unfriendly region is the village of Matmata, where pockets of date palms and subterranean houses barely make a mark on the landscape.

The man-made craters of the village's adaptive homes, dug some twenty to twenty-five feet deep into the earth, function as center courtyards for each house. Dug into the sides of the courtyard are rooms hollowed out of the earth. Ceilings are sometimes chiseled into dome and vault shapes for added structural strength. Exterior courtyard walls are either faced with limestone blocks, plaster, and whitewash or left raw and exposed.

The women of the village do most of their chores in the courtyards, until the heat drives them back inside to the cool recesses of the earth. The physical and social adaptations of the people of Matmata to the harsh demands of their environment are not unlike those of the many desert animals who build burrows underneath the scorching surface of the desert to keep themselves cool and maintain stable temperatures.

DJERBA

LEFT: A BLUE MOSQUE DOORWAY SIGNIFIES GOOD LUCK.

RIGHT: THERE ARE MORE THAN TWO HUNDRED MOSQUES ON THE SMALL ISLAND OF DJERBA. BUTTRESSES SUPPORT THE MASSIVE STONE WALLS, AND SMALL OPENINGS KEEP THE INTERIORS COOL. WHITEWASH CREATES A REFLECTIVE EXTERIOR AND A LIGHT INTERIOR.

T he island of Djerba, which is claimed to be the famed isle of the lotus-eaters in Homer's *Odyssey*, is a flat land off the southeastern coast of Tunisia where clusters of prickly pear cacti, agaves, palms, figs, and olive trees grow. Mosques punctuate the landscape.

The architecture of the island incorporates the use of barrel vaults and domes that flow into long white walls with small windows. The windows, often trimmed in bright blue, a color believed to bring good luck, provide ventilation and allow direct shafts of sunlight to penetrate and illuminate highly reflective white interiors. Thick walls made from earth or stone insulate against the heat of the day and the cool of the night. Exterior layers of worn whitewashed walls blend into the surrounding colors of sand. Offshore, small brightly painted wooden fishing boats rock back and forth in the rolling surf where curlews and oyster catchers dance to the rhythm of the waves.

At the northern end of the island is the city of Houmt Souk, the capital of Djerba, where the old lends harmonizing inspiration to the new. Concrete tries to imitate stone and adobe, but cannot compete with their ability to retain a stable temperature. New resorts that snuggle up to pristine beaches house the year-round influx of tourists, using classical lines but not traditional mate-

TOP: SCARCITY OF WOOD
RESULTS IN AN ARCHITECTURE
DOMINATED BY LIMESTONE
DOMES AND VAULTS.

BOTTOM: THE VARIED
ELEVATIONS OF THE LONG
MOSQUE WALLS BLEND INTO
THE LANDSCAPE OF SAND
AND SEA.

rials. Just inland from the beach is the city center, where hand-loomed Berber carpets in bold geometric patterns and colors hang from the white walls and covered walkways of the rug merchants.

The main streets are filled with pedestrians, trucks, buses, and cars. Horns honk, brakes squeak, and people shout at one another, shaking their fists wildly in the air. Tall white walls are built close together to

create shade and relief from the sun. Arab women draped in yards of fabric seem to float through passageways, leaving behind a suggestion of forbidden mystery. And everywhere high-pitched melodic music permeates the air.

From the mosque, five times a day, chants of the muezzin, or "Allah's messenger," call the people to prayer over a loudspeaker. Men in djellabas, long loose-fitting tunics that protect them from exposure to the harmful rays of the sun and slow down the rate of evaporation, leave what they are doing to go to the mosque and recite prayers, always with their prayer mats facing east toward Mecca, the holy city. In the evening, everything winds down to the slow motion of the *schicha*, or water pipe, that is filled with a special tobacco and openly smoked by many of the men in the yellowish light of the public cafés or on street corners in the dark recesses of a doorway. Night brings a welcome silence as the city withdraws behind high walls and enters a state of deep sleep.

A number of small white villages dot the eastern coastline of Djerba. Houses are surrounded by fences of prickly pear and long low rambling walls, behind which grow date palms. Beneath the trees, carefully guarded from the searing heat of the day, garden vegetables grow — made possible by the open canals that bring water from the community well or spring.

Several houses are built with triangular-shaped parapets at either end and a long barrel vault in between. Others, with intersecting vaults, resemble a Greek cross. Homes with flat roofs use split palm trunks as roof supports, the only usable wood on the island other than small amounts of olive. This lack of lumber accounts for some of the innovative styles that have developed over the centuries. The soft edges of these structures produce the illusion of form and landscape melting into each other. For example, a small mosque stands adjacent to the water's edge. Its curving architectural lines are created by the irregular surfaces of its domes and vaults. Walls, supported by impressive buttresses made with sharp angles, are the color of vanilla and seem to dissolve into a background of clouds and sand. The mosque has only minimal impact on the environment, yet functions successfully as a public space.

KASBAH OF AÏT BENHADDOU

Not far south of Marrakesh in Morocco, a flat barren landscape littered with chunks of gypsum lies against a background of spongy-looking pastel pink and yellow hills. Blended in with these soft earthen mounds is the old Kasbah, or fortress, in the town of Aït Benhaddou. Mud walls surround and fortify the Kasbah and help keep out the strong chilling winds that sweep down from the Atlas Mountains. In the center of the Kasbah is a crumbling synagogue that was built by a population of Jewish refugees who were expelled from Spain in 1492. Today, there are only seven Jewish families left in the village; the rest have migrated to Israel or other sympathetic nations.

Sheltered by the fortresslike exterior of the Kasbah are high multistoried walls of earth, with crenellated corner towers and few windows. The walls provide shade because of their close proximity, as well as a pallette for sculpted wall reliefs. These structures form multiple-housing compounds that are clustered and attached by common walls. Covered passageways, leading in and around the maze of buildings, create additional shade and an outdoor place to exchange conversation with neighbors and friends.

An interior complex may house several families and will have storage areas and animal enclosures that open onto a central

LEFT: THE FERTILE MOROCCAN LOWLANDS ARE RESERVED FOR GARDENS IN AÏT BENHADDOU.

RIGHT: GEOMETRIC DESIGNS DECORATE MUD-PLASTERED WALL SURFACES.

courtyard. Inside, massive walls maintain stable temperatures, as in a freestanding cave. Ventilation is provided through high windows and square corner towers, which open up to the outside, drawing out the heat and capturing cool breezes.

Outside the walls of the Kasbah, beside the Drâa River, are extensive gardens of dates, figs, other fruit trees, grains, and vegetables, made possible by the constant supply of water.

The Kasbah of Aït Benhaddou is well camouflaged by its repetitive design elements that mimic the surrounding environ-

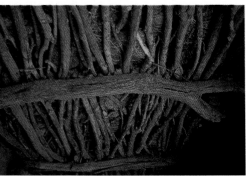

ment. Because it is a compact community huddled against a hillside, residents are assured of a safe location out of the river basin during torrential downpours, while the fertile lowlands are reserved for cultivation. The overall design provides a comfortable habitat in an extremely challenging climate, as well as a strategic location for defense.

TOP: PROTECTIVE MUD WALLS SURROUND AND FORTIFY THE KASBAH AT AÏT BENHADDOU. TO AVOID THE FLOOD-PRONE AREAS AND FOR DEFENSE, RESIDENTS CONSTRUCT HOUSES ON THE SIDES OF THE HILLS. THIS MULTIPLE-HOUSING COMPLEX RESEMBLES HOUSES OF THE EARLIER PUEBLO INDIANS IN NORTH AMERICA.

BOTTOM: THE CEILING STRUCTURE OF A ROOM IN THE KASBAH OF AÏT BENHADDOU IS BUILT WITH INDIGENOUS MATERIALS.

THE COMPACT COMMUNITY OF
AÏT BENHADDOU HAS BUILT-IN
OUTDOOR SITTING AREAS. ITS
TUNNELED CORRIDORS PROVIDE
SHADE FROM THE SUMMER SUN.

DRÂA RIVER VALLEY

LEFT: DOORWAYS CAST
SHADOWS THAT HELP SHADE
ENTRANCES.

RIGHT: IN THE LABYRINTH OF
PASSAGEWAYS THAT WEAVE
AROUND THE KASBAH GLAOUI
TAOURIRT, ROOF DRAINS CAN
BE SEEN. THEY ARE CARVED OUT
OF THE SIDES OF THE WALLS
AND FINISHED WITH CEMENT
PLASTER, ENABLING WATER TO
SPILL DOWN THE SIDES
WITHOUT ERODING THE ADOBE.

The Drâa River flows south as it heads for the edge of the Sahara in Morocco. Beyond Ouarzazate, ridges of land, sculpted by the flow of the river, fan out in circular patterns like ripples of water. Fossil beds from an ancient sea that covered most of the Sahara more than four hundred million years ago contain trilobites and goniatites — fossils that are collected and sold by the local population. A backdrop of jagged rock zigzags across the desert like sleeping Chinese dragons. As the valley opens, following the course of the river, crumbling walls of old Kasbahs rise above the earth. Their mud walls match the colors of the soil, which change from mile to mile.

Hills of muted yellow meet and merge with those colored in pinks and dark rust, then lavender and gray-white. Some areas are built up with soft clays, while others are paved with bronze pebbles that have been burnished by the sun and wind. All looks empty and forsaken. Only an occasional circle of palms breaks up the monotony.

In the village of Aït Saoun, the buildings have elaborate parapets and pointed arches that are pinched in at the middle, a style that traveled with the Moors across the Mediterranean into southern Spain. The town ends abruptly, surrounded by more rocks and empty space.

The town of Tamnougait skirts the

TOP: SOUTHERN MOROCCAN VILLAGES ARE FILLED WITH MUD TOWERS, MINARETS, AND ADOBE WALLS. INTRICATE DESIGNS AND SHAPES EMBELLISH EXTERIOR SURFACES.

BOTTOM: IN RURAL AREAS OF MOROCCO, THE PEOPLE MAKE THEIR OWN ADOBES OUT OF LOCAL SOIL AND LAY THEM ON THE GROUND TO DRY.

riverbanks. The village exterior is defined only by horizontal ribbons of rust-colored walls and the clay-colored earth. Huge adobe structures with minimal openings to the street provide privacy and buffer the interiors from strong winds that bring in clouds of dust. Interior courtyards and terraces are screened from the streets by high enclosing walls. It is here that the women enjoy the light and warmth of the open sky without venturing into the public eye. Domestic gardens are limited to potted plants on the roof terrace, a spreading shade tree, and a few shrubs in the center court.

In the village, lines of wet adobe are laid out to dry. Bundles of reed that will be used to span ceilings between beams rest against house walls. Inside the houses, a sanctuary of earthen walls keeps the air cool and refreshing. Entries tend to be formal places reserved for receiving the public, but closed off from the private living spaces. In the cen-

tral living areas plastered walls can be two stories high. Overhead, windcatchers, ingenious four-sided adobe boxes with open sides, catch the breezes, ventilate the hot air, and let in a muted light.

The mud village of Ouiad Driss is composed of vertical towers and minarets covered by patterns sculpted into the mud plaster. Tunneled streets are interrupted by openings where shafts of light pierce dark interiors. Women stand in the cool recesses of their doorways talking with one another, invisible to the outside world. As in many other villages in the area, tall exterior walls made from rammed earth have only high small openings, used for ventilation and small amounts of light. Above and beyond the view from the street, ringed by high parapet walls, are sleeping porches and roof gardens.

The last village in the Drâa River valley before the Sahara is M'hamid, a military outpost made up of modern buildings that emulate more classical forms — traditional brown walls and soft corners instead of the hard edges of the contemporary world. The streets of the town are filling with sand from the encroaching desert beyond, a region of shifting dunes and rock-covered plains. Date palm fronds are woven together in a honeycomb pattern to prevent the drifting sand from covering the highway. The blue-veiled men, known as Tuareg ("Tuareg" is an Arabic name meaning "abandoned by God"), are also moving into the town. These people were originally nomadic, surviving by herding goats and sheep, as well as pillaging from other tribes and villages. But now, as the desert continues to swallow up land, and water holes dry out, Tuareg are forced to turn to a lifestyle that has never been part of their heritage — town life.

RIGHT: WALLS SOUTHEAST OF THE ATLAS MOUNTAINS HELP PROTECT STRUCTURES FROM THE STRONG WINDS AND KEEP OUT BLOWING SAND.

MARRAKESH

LEFT: BLANK WALLS RUN THE
LENGTH OF THE STREETS IN
MARRAKESH, BROKEN UP BY
DECORATIVE DOORWAYS THAT
IDENTIFY THE INHABITANTS.

RIGHT: THE FRUIT FROM THE
PRICKLY PEAR CACTUS IS
CONSIDERED A DELICACY AND
IS SOLD IN LOCAL MARKETS OR
SOUKS OFF CARTS PULLED
THROUGH THE STREETS.

The snowcapped Atlas Mountains of Morocco and a dense forest of palm trees frame the ancient city of Marrakesh, also known as Marrakesh the Red, a name derived from the matching red color of the earth, walls, and buildings. Founded in the eleventh century, the city is revered for its elaborate gardens, spraying fountains, and historic monuments, all made possible by a network of ancient underground canals that provide the city with water.

Jamâa el-Fna, the city square where tentacles from the local souk, or market, overtake the central district, is in many ways the heart of this great oasis. Small cubicles stuffed with merchandise are crammed together, one next to another in a row of stalls that share common partitions and are connected by narrow aisles and roads. A dizzying collection of items are sold — fresh fruits and vegetables; colorful herbs and spices, including saffron flowers, turmeric, curry, and ginger; and brassware, jewelry, rugs, djellabas, cassette tapes, shoes, purses, hats, miniature stuffed camels, water jugs made from recycled tires. Colorfully clad snake charmers, acrobats, musicians, and fire-eaters entertain spectators throughout the day and night. This city is in constant flux, teeming with life.

Although the traditional vernacular architecture is slowly vanishing in favor of new

LEFT: Intricate patterns on, above, and to the sides of doorways make entrances most impressive.

RIGHT: Ornate grillwork covers openings and provides privacy, but does not interfere with airflow.

high-rise buildings, now silhouetted against the horizon, just beyond the marketplace old, high, rose-colored walls follow the length of the streets. Recessed doorways, elaborately ornamented, punctuate the lower portions of facades, while intimate windows covered with latticework screens for privacy decorate the upper stories. Houses face inward, their rooms surrounding courtyards with small formal gardens containing fountains, trees, and flowers. Interior spaces are embellished with intricate patterns incised into the plaster and woodwork, an ancient art form that developed during the twelfth through the fourteenth centuries. Colorful tiles decorate stairways and walls with interlacing designs of com-

plex patterns, mirroring the bright, rich landscape.

The smell of incense lingers in doorways, and resonant sounds of sweet music filter through the openings. Above this are the voices of women, laughing and talking behind the high walls, traditionally hidden from the rest of the world in their islands of sanctuary. Today, not all women in Marrakesh remain behind the walls of their homes. Many have become westernized, shedding their traditional clothing for more contemporary styles, hair loose and veils gone.

Reflecting the evolution of the culture, the architecture of Marrakesh also has become somewhat westernized. Modern concrete skyscrapers and highrises contrast with the traditional adobe buildings. Marrakesh has become a city where new and old worlds exist side by side.

SOUTHERN SPAIN

outhern Spain is a land of contrasts, ranging from low-lands and river valleys to coastal plains and badlands, with mountain peaks rising more than eleven thousand feet. The long ridges are split by deep canyons and gullies. The climate varies from over eight months of snowfall in the higher elevations to temperatures reaching well above a hundred degrees Fahrenheit on the southern slopes and lowlands. Over the centuries, Phoenicians, Vandals, Visigoths, Romans, Moors, and Christians have inhabited southern Spain, surviving and adapting, as well as contributing some of the finest examples of architecture in this part of the world.

The cities are intoxicating places, packed with sights, sounds, and smells that reach back into centuries of history. Old and new coexist in this region where the architecture changed with each new conqueror.

Many rural areas have been left unchanged. Their narrow cobbled streets still follow the contours of the landscape, and their limestone slopes provide the building blocks of local homes. Outside the villages, ancient canals are visible and in many cases are still in use.

The Sierra Morena, a long range of low mountains at the southern end of Spain's central plateau, or Meseta, separates southern Spain from the rest of the country. The Meseta reaches more than 2,500 feet in elevation before ending

ABOVE: THE TOWN OF CASARES IS PERCHED ON TOP OF A ROCKY HILL-TOP, A LOCATION THAT IS EASY TO DEFEND. DURING INVASIONS IN THE MIDDLE AGES, PEOPLE WOULD GATHER IN THE FORTRESS FOR SAFETY.

BELOW: PAST CIVILIZATIONS OF SPAIN CAN BE TRACED THROUGH ARCHITECTURAL ORNAMENTATION. THE FORTRESS OF ALMODÓVAR DEL RIO HAS DETAILS DATING FROM SEVERAL PERIODS, INCLUDING THE TIMES OF THE ROMANS AND MOORS.

PRECEDING PAGES: BRIDGES FROM ROMAN AND ARAB TIMES SPAN THE R. GUADALEVÍN IN THE TOWN OF RONDA.

abruptly as a series of folds that flank the Guadalquivir, a triangular lowland or plain considered to be the beginning of Andalucia. Dominating the plain is the Guadalquivir River, which cuts through and around several major cities, including Córdoba and Sevilla. Beyond the northeastern end of the triangle, the plain changes to arid badlands marked by barren hills, open spaces, and thin soils incapable of supporting much in the way of vegetation. Rich mineral content seems obvious by the horizontal banding of colors, including gray, rouge, and tawny beige. Farther west the earth changes to more productive farmland, where limestone, chalk, clay, and sand combine as a base for a top coat of fertile soil. Parts of this region have been under cultivation for over three thousand years.

The middle and lower Guadalquivir is open and flat, broken up by an occasional hill or small ravine. The Moors, who occupied southern Spain from 711 to 1492, devised irrigation systems and a series of canals from the river to the fields.

South of the Guadalquivir is the Sierra Nevada, an impres-

sive range of granite and limestone mountains with steep gorges that extends from Granada to Almería. The highest point, often covered in snow and ice, is more than 11,400 feet. Dramatic cliffs sweep down to the Mediterranean and onto several coastal plains. Sheep graze on the grasses of the upper elevations, while farming dominates the lower slopes.

Hundreds of small villages in southern Spain — such as Orgiva, located off the Guadalfeo drainage — reflect the ingenuity and adaptability of its people to the challenges of this arid environment. Stone houses butt up to cliff faces, reminiscent of Anasazi dwellings. Like the Anasazi homes, many of southern Spain's cave houses are abandoned, but their architecture remains as a testament to their acclimatization. Not

far from Orgiva, clusters of houses stand on terraced cliffs. Stone walls, held together with clay mortar, are capped with slate from nearby hills. Close by, older homes, with new solar collectors on their rooftops, are set into shallow pockets between south-facing hillsides.

Around the cultivated fields in southern Spain are acres of rolling hills dotted with olive trees and ringed by mountain

ranges, with stair-step terraces on their slopes. Houses are often built directly into the hillsides, taking advantage of the natural insulation of the earth and limestone. Still encircling the fields are stone walls dating from the Moors' occupation

ABOVE: GYPSY CAVE DWELLINGS ARE ON HOLY HILL IN GRANADA. ROOMS ARE HOLLOWED OUT OF THE LIMESTONE HILLS, WHOSE MASS PROVIDES INSULATION FROM THE SUMMER HEAT. (PHOTO BY SUZI MOORE)

LEFT: THE VILLAGE OF LUCAINENA ON THE RIO ADRA IS IN THE SOUTHERN SIERRA NEVADA, WHERE MANY OF THE MOORS WENT INTO HIDING AFTER THEY WERE EXILED IN 1492. TERRACES WITH LOW ROCK WALLS BUILT BY THE MOORS ARE STILL USED FOR FARMING TODAY.

of the land. Crops include grapes, peaches, cereal grains, citrus, cotton, and garden vegetables. Southern Spain has become a productive region because of the efforts by generations of Spaniards, who have overcome numerous challenges presented to them by the arid climate and landscape.

ABANDONED CAVE HOUSES

Not too far from the town of Baza, the land levels out with only a few rounded knolls rising from the earth. Expansive gray skies blend with brown grasses, gray-green scrub, and sporadic trees. Higher hills are off in the distance to the east. To the west the land is uninterrupted.

Dug into a south-facing draw hidden by the earth and chaparral is an abandoned community of cave dwellings. Shallow trenches, most likely used for irrigation, skirt the perimeter. Chiseled out of the soft earth are U-shaped houses with their main entrances facing south. Walls are up to five feet thick, and ceilings are vault shaped in order to support the load they need to carry. Un-like cave dwellings in other dry areas in southern Spain, walls and ceilings in some of the interior rooms are also coated with transparent washes of raw umber or vivid blue.

Main living rooms branch off into side rooms and hollowed-out sleeping alcoves that reach far into the interior of the hillside. Some of the more elaborate dwellings have up to ten rooms burrowed into the earth. An open fire pit for cooking, vented by conical chimneys that climb through twenty feet of earth before emerging, is located in the kitchen area. Many rooftops are flat circular areas paved with cobblestones, possibly used for communal gatherings.

CORTES

LEFT: THE CAVE HOMES OF CORTES ARE CARVED INTO THE HILLS AND THEN WHITEWASHED INSIDE AND OUT. THE MASS OF EARTH HELPS STABILIZE THE TEMPERATURE INSIDE. CHILIES ARE HUNG ON THE OUTSIDE WALLS, AND ONIONS AND SQUASH ARE LAID OUT ON THE GROUND TO DRY COMPLETELY BEFORE THEY ARE PUT INTO STORAGE INSIDE THE CAVES.

RIGHT: DOORWAYS, WINDOWS, AND FACADES OF THE CAVE HOMES ARE CARVED DIRECTLY OUT OF THE EARTH.

Among the hills of southern Spain are communities that may date as far back as the Iberian occupation in 600 B.C. Crowning many of these hill towns are old stone fortress walls, reminders of more than seven centuries of Moorish rule.

Many of the villages, set into sides of hills or against rock faces with massive stone overhangs, follow the natural contours of the land and are thus sheltered from the brutal effects of direct sun and wind. Built from insulating materials such as limestone, brick, or earth, these homes often share a common wall and form a close-knit community with little need to rely on motorized transportation.

The houses of Cortes, a town east of Granada, are hollowed out of eroded hillsides. Chimneys or ventilation stacks reach up and out from the earth. Facades are sculpted into flat surfaces and coated with lime stucco to seal and protect the delicate earthen walls. Door and window openings — some with contemporary wrought-iron doors and grillwork — are carved into walls three to four feet thick. Most of the houses have television antennas protruding from the earthen rooftops. Often roads will cross directly over a portion of a roof, which is composed of eight feet of earth, with clusters of prickly pear cacti and other shrubs, planted to hold on to the precious soils.

Cortes, an agricultural community, reserves the productive lowlands down by the river for farming and maintains residences on the hillsides away from the floodplain.

The people of Cortes believe their houses to be superior to contemporary structures made from high-tech materials and boast about the stable year-round temperature provided by thick walls of earth or limestone. Ceilings are sculpted into dome shapes for structural support, and interior walls are coated with the same lime stucco used on the exterior in order to reflect the limited sunlight that enters. The kitchen is generally a large room located off to one side, with a chimney over the cooking area to draw the smoke up and away from the hillside. Most of the houses are meticulously finished and provide comfortable living spaces.

ABOVE: ABANDONED CAVE HOMES BECOME ANIMAL ENCLOSURES AND STORAGE AREAS.

RIGHT: THESE OLD CAVE DWELLINGS ARE USED FOR STORING CROPS.

MONTEFRIO

LEFT: DUG INTO THE SIDES OF CLIFFS, HOUSES IN MONTEFRIO ARE WHITE AND HAVE BURROWED ROOMS TO HELP INSULATE THE INTERIORS FROM THE HEAT AND COLD.

RIGHT: THE HOUSES ARE CONSTRUCTED WITH INDIGENOUS MATERIALS. EARTH AND STONE ARE USED FOR WALLS, AND FIRED CLAY FOR ROOFS. BECAUSE OF THE INHERENT MOISTURE IN THE CLAY, IT IS NOT UNUSUAL TO SEE LICHEN-COVERED ROOFS SPROUTING TUFTS OF GRASS.

Northwest of Granada is a landscape of olive orchards and freshly plowed hillsides. In the river valley, grape arbors spread out, engulfing the houses in a sea of green that keeps them in shade during the hotter seasons. At times the structures appear to be swallowed up by an entire field, exposing only a portion of the roof and maybe a chimney stack.

Wrapped around one of the hillsides is the town of Montefrio. Houses in classic geometric patterns of white on white, topped with red tile roofs, follow the contours of the natural landscape. A number of houses are attached to the hillsides, hollowed directly out of limestone. Others hang suspended from ridges, like swallows' nests. Colorfully patterned fabrics shade doorways of the densely packed houses. Grape arbors that provide shade during the hot season allow the sun to penetrate the homes in the winter, when the vines lose their leaves.

At the base of a steep incline, in one of the houses carved into a limestone hill, lives ninety-six-year-old Dolores Mazuela Silvera. She has lived in Montefrio her entire life. Her one-bedroom house is surrounded by white-walled flower beds filled with bright red geraniums. It is typical of many in the village. The house is always cool in the summer and warm in the winter due to its thick stone walls, which are partially

buried in the hillside. Both the interior and exterior walls have been covered with coats of traditional plaster and whitewash. Inside, a front sitting room is decorated simply with a table, several straight-backed chairs, and family pictures hanging from walls. Natural light pours in from the doorway and a small window, illuminating the front room. In the farther recesses of the hillside, a small bedroom has been hollowed out of the rock, providing enough space for a double bed and nightstand. A spiral stairway, also carved into the limestone, is hidden in one corner and leads to a storage area. The back bedroom

TOP: STONE WALLS AND CLAY-TILE ROOFS BLEND WITH THE NATURAL TERRAIN. HOUSES FOLLOW THE CONTOURS OF THE LANDSCAPE.

BOTTOM: STEPS BUILT INTO A HILL LEAD UP TO A CHURCH, WHICH WAS CONSTRUCTED AMID THE RUINS OF A MOORISH FORTRESS.

PRECEDING PAGES: HOUSES ARE NESTLED BETWEEN SLOPES IN THIS MOUNTAINOUS REGION OF SOUTHERN SPAIN. OLIVE TREES LINE THE ROLLING HILLS SURROUNDING MONTEFRIO.

barely receives any light. "But," as Dolores points out, "this is not important, since the room is only used for sleeping."

As generations pass, changes take place, but the climate, landscape, and availability of native materials still dictate what the local architecture will look like.

Earth and stone are used for walls and fired clay for roofs—materials that provide superior insulation while still in keeping with the landscape of Montefrio and its traditional architecture. Standing on top of a hill is an old stone church and the remains of ancient fortress walls built from limestone.

Down below, on a side street off the main plaza, is a Romanesque-style limestone building. Around window openings blocks of stone have been beveled outward to allow a greater amount of sunlight to enter. Limestone is still one of the dominant features in the surrounding landscape and an obvious choice for local construction. Many freestanding structures use rectangular blocks of this plentiful rock, shaped by men in the community who work only with hammers and chisels.

CÓRDOBA

On the Andalusian Plain, long stretches of agricultural lands fill the landscape surrounding the city of Córdoba. Mixed in with fields of cereal grains, cotton, and citrus are old haciendas, or self-sufficient compounds, with mature eucalyptus trees used for windscreens, historic white villages with castles crowning their hilltops, olive orchards that form shimmering rows of silver across the upper plains, and small farmhouses with grape arbors attached to their southern facades. Skies are open and expansive, filled with a brilliant white light. Long, winding streets lead to the core of the inner city. This is where the true character of the once-Islamic capital of Andalucía begins to reveal itself.

Plazas, courtyards, and gardens are the essence of the Córdoba of both yesterday and today, supplying open spaces in an otherwise closed-in city. The public *placitas*, or small squares, skirted by shade trees and shops, serve as a welcome break between the narrow streets, which provide much-needed shade from the blazing sun but can feel claustrophobic. Cafes open onto plazas and streets—their chairs and small tables line the narrow sidewalks.

Houses are designed to turn inward, just as their predecessors did in North Africa, adaptively creating havens from the outside world with rooms surrounded by private

LEFT: LA MEZQUITA, THE GREAT MOSQUE OF CÓRDOBA, WAS BUILT ON THE SITE OF AN OLD VISIGOTH CHURCH BETWEEN A.D. 780 AND 785 BY ABD AL-RAHMAN I. THE MIHRAB, OR HOLY SANCTUARY, FACES MECCA TO GUIDE WORSHIPERS IN THE DIRECTION OF PRAYER. THE DOME, COVERED WITH MOSAICS AND TILES, IS RESPLENDENT.

RIGHT: COVERED IN SHEETS OF BRONZE, THE GATES OF PARDON ON THE NORTH END OF LA MEZQUITA WERE NAMED FOLLOWING A PARDONING OF PENITENTS IN FRONT OF THEM. THE DOORS AND KNOCKERS DATE FROM THE FOURTEENTH CENTURY.

courtyards and patios. These intimate oases, filled with stone fountains, climbing vines of bougainvillea, and potted flowers, offer not only a retreat but a connection with the natural elements of light, air, water, and native plants.

The architectural influences of past civilizations in southern Spain are easily tracked by the ornate and contrasting design of La Mezquita. It is the world's third-largest mosque, built by Abd al-Rahman I during A.D. 780 to 785 on the site of an old Visigoth church that was once a Roman temple. The imposing exterior is a faded brown, built of long limestone walls covered with plaster. The entrances are adorned with ornate plasterwork, tracery in floral patterns, and horseshoe arches. The Patio de los Narajos, or Patio of the Orange Grove, leads into an unexpected forest of columns supporting double arches banded with ochre and rust. Elaborate Corinthian capitals top pillars of marble, granite, and onyx salvaged from Roman and Visigoth ruins. Even though there were several expansions over a period of time, each section flows into the other,

ISLAMIC INFLUENCES ARE OBVIOUS IN MUCH OF THE ARCHITECTURE IN CÓRDOBA.

some with intricate arches that are lobed or inverted, others with paired or branching columns.

As a whole there is a logical sequence among the sections that continues with un-interrupted rhythm until the center of the mosque, where an awkward mass rises. In 1523, almost three hundred years after Córdoba fell to the Christians, construction began on a Baroque cathedral in the center of the mosque. More than sixty columns and some of the finest decorative panels of plas-terwork were removed and most of the en-trances sealed up, insensitive to the light and air that once easily moved through the mosque, making its interior as welcome and cool a retreat as the city's many plazas and patios. Despite the irreparable damage, the mosque remains the pride of the city and the most resplendent example of the domi-nant Islamic architecture.

SEVILLA

LEFT: TWIN COLUMNS SUPPORT ELABORATE, MULTILOBED ARCHES IN THE COURTYARD OF THE MAIDENS AT THE REALES ALCÁZARES DE SEVILLA. THE WALLS ARE DECORATED WITH SOME OF THE ORIGINAL FOURTEENTH-CENTURY TILES AND DELICATE PLASTERWORK CARVED WITH INTRICATE ORNAMENTATION. EVEN THE SOFFITS ARE EMBELLISHED.

RIGHT: INTRICATE TILE WORK, LOBED ARCHES, AND DELICATE RELIEF ADORN THE WALLS AND COLONNADES AT THE REALES ALCÁZARES. THE COURTYARD IS AN EXAMPLE OF MUDEJAR, A MUSLIM-CHRISTIAN ARCHITEC-TURAL STYLE.

The center of Sevilla began with a mosque and a minaret. The minaret was used by the muezzin, who sang out the call to prayer, and served as a landmark for those unfamiliar with the city. Eventually, the mosque was converted into one of the largest Gothic cathedrals in the world, and the minaret, La Giralda, was rebuilt and capped with a Gothic top and spire.

Across from La Giralda and the cathedral is the Reales Alcázares (or Real Alcázar), Sevilla's royal palace. The original structure is believed to have been built on the site of an old Roman citadel and was used primarily as a residence for Moorish kings during the twelfth century. Later,

during the fourteenth century, the Alcázar underwent major remodeling, resulting in an architecture known as the Mudejar style, which combines both Muslim and Christian influences.

In the Alcázar, a string of patios and enclosed courtyards with arched colonnades and marble floors leads into a vast labyrinth of interior rooms and hallways decorated with elaborate tile and woodwork, paintings, and ornate ceramic pieces. Corinthian capitals top marble columns that support intricate arches covered in relief. Coffered ceilings are embellished with layers of woodwork that have inlaid geometric designs highlighted in gold leaf and polychromes.

Outside, breezes blow across pools of water, producing an effect equivalent to that of a giant evaporative cooler and a relaxing atmosphere where palace residents could sit in contemplation.

From La Giralda, a tangled web of narrow streets and passageways leads away from the *medina*, or city center, the heart of Sevilla, and winds around, creating mazelike patterns that eventually meet at *placitas*, or small squares, lined by outdoor cafés, fruit trees, and stone fountains. The random street layout helps ensure privacy, a relished commodity. Heavy wrought-iron gates stand closed, but behind them doors remain open. One residence appears to melt into another, the line between them indistinct. Plain facades are broken up by wooden doors and elaborate wrought-iron latticework that cover window openings and act as balcony railings. Inside the houses, *zaguanes*, or covered breezeways, open onto courtyards washed in soft shades of color. Elaborate gardens with carved stone fountains are surrounded by wraparound *portales*, or covered porches, that have sets of double doors leading into interior living spaces. Red flowers in ornate containers line the balconies.

More than just shade providers, the gardens are an integral part of Islamic tradition and architecture. The Moors believed gardens to be places of contemplation, as dictated by the Koran, where one could sit and meditate and be refreshed by the sound of water while being spiritually renewed, an area symbolizing paradise on earth.

NARROW PASSAGEWAYS, OR
CALLEJONES, FAN OUT FROM THE
CENTER OF SEVILLA. THE
CLOSENESS OF THE WALLS, AS IN
THE KASBAHS IN MOROCCO,
CREATES SHADE.

GRANADA

G ranada, fabled land of epic poems, lyrical songs, imaginative stories, and fanciful art, was the last of the Muslim cities to fall into the hands of the Christians, in 1492.

Situated at the northern base of the snowcapped Sierra Nevada and stretching out across the high plain, today Granada is crammed full of cars, people, winding roads, and buildings. Despite the haze of pollution lingering in the air, Granada still exudes an exotic appeal, based more on its past than its present. This appeal emanates from the Alhambra, or Oal'at al-Hamra, meaning "red fort" in Arabic, which presides over the city from its strategic hillside location. With its expansive gardens and memorable architecture, the Alhambra is a tribute to and confirmation of the achievements attained during the seven centuries of Granada's occupation by the Moors. Gates and gardens lead the way into the main complex, where rooms open onto rectangular courtyards with center pools and fountains. The pools act as cooling components and mirror the encircling architecture, expanding the elevations to whimsical proportions. The repetition of columns and the constantly changing light and shadow further the illusion of movement. Delicate stuccowork, known as *muqarnas*, is used on ceilings and walls, creating the illusion of three-dimensional space,

while designs using mosaics, stucco, and wood take shape as geometric designs, inscriptions, and floral ornamentation.

Below the Alhambra is the Albaicín, the nucleus of the old city, where only a few fragmented pieces of the Arab kingdom still exist. The narrow winding roads lined with whitewashed walls suggest another world, one of mosques and gardens, fountains and pools, Arab baths, and the original royal court. Several Arab buildings remain intact, but most of them are gone, along with the troglodyte community on the hill north of the Alhambra known as Sacromonte, or

Holy Hill. Gypsies still occupy a few of the remaining cave houses, first inhabited by the Visigoths, and then later by the Moors, but many were abandoned in 1962 when major flooding destroyed most of the community.

Granada is a mix of cultures, including those of the Phoenicians, Iberians, Romans, Visigoths, and Moors. Religion often played a major role in the exchange of old for new. When the Moors invaded Spain in 711, Visigoth churches and Roman temples were torn down and replaced by mosques. When the Christians conquered the Moors in 1492, the landscape and architecture both changed

ABOVE: THE ALHAMBRA IS STRATEGICALLY LOCATED ON A HILL OVERLOOKING GRANADA. BUILT BY THE MOORS, THE CASTLE ASSUMED GREAT IMPORTANCE DURING THE EARLY 1200S. ORIGINALLY, THE ASABICA, OR TOP OF THE HILL, WAS CUT IN HALF BY A RAVINE THAT WAS LATER FILLED IN BY THE CHRISTIANS.

PRECEDING PAGES: FLOWERING VINES AND SHRUBS ADD A SPLASH OF VIOLET TO THE COURTYARDS AND GARDENS AT THE ALHAMBRA.

dramatically. A ravine originally divided the asabica, or the top of the hill where the Alhambra stands. When the Christians conquered Spain they filled in the ravine and razed the mosques, replacing them with cathedrals. Today the process continues — woven together are old and new, sharp lines and soft edges, narrow streets and wide boulevards. The diversity creates a unique city of great architectural importance.

NATIVE AMERICA

variety of dry deserts make up the landscape of the southwestern U.S. and Mexico, a landscape that has played host to numerous Indian tribes over thousands of years. In southern Arizona and New Mexico the inhospitable Basin and Range is a region of baked earth filled with thorns and spiny plants. In the summer, raging thunderstorms tear at the earth, flooding the valleys and moving soils downstream. The summer heat seems endless; the winters are mild.

The Colorado Plateau extends its landscape throughout the Four Corners, which includes southeastern Utah, northeastern Arizona, northwestern New Mexico, and southwestern Colorado. The region is highlighted by sandstone canyons, mesas, buttes, and spires. It is a land with little fertile soil, a land where grasses and chaparral plants have a precarious hold on the terrain. The winters can be cold and harsh, while the summers last just long enough to plant and harvest.

ABOVE: At Paquimé, or the Casas Grandes ruins, in Chihuahua, Mexico, a mixture of techniques was used for constructing the walls, including pisé, wattle and daub, and mud-laid stones.

LEFT: Paquimé, or Casas Grandes, was a large village six and seven stories high. Occupation dates are debatable, but most recently Dr. Ben Brown has speculated that Paquimé thrived between a.d. 1300 and 1450.

BELOW: Built between a.d. 950 and 1050, Pueblo Bonito was probably the largest Anasazi site in Chaco Canyon, in present-day New Mexico, housing possibly a thousand people in more than one hundred rooms. Wooden beams indicate that a forest was nearby. Today the soils are thin and the rainfall scarce.

Western Texas and southwestern New Mexico stretch north into the High Plains, where grasslands dominate the soils.

PRECEDING PAGES: Occupation at Mesa Verde in southwestern Colorado can be traced back to a.d. 600, although it was not until 1150 that elaborate, multistoried complexes were built. Square Tower House is one example of many showing the skilled masonry work of the Anasazi Indians.

Clusters of mesquite trees help shade the burning earth. The summers can be unbearable, turning the earth to a crusted brown, until the rains arrive to renew the land.

For many years the indigenous peoples adapted to this land characterized by erratic cycles of drought and floods. They were nomads, following animal herds, finding or building temporary shelters, and moving on when their food supplies were low. Around 500 B.C., corn was introduced, creating a dramatic cultural revolution, one that spread across the Southwest, causing nomadic hunters and gatherers to turn to a settled way of life. Corn inspired the Indians to develop dry-farming techniques along with ingenious methods of capturing runoff and building canals to irrigate fields.

As agriculture gained in importance, so did native architecture. The first dwellings were rudimentary — simple dugouts covered with brush. Eventually more elaborate structures were built. Underground shelters were redefined as storage rooms and kivas, or ceremonial chambers. Between A.D. 1100 and 1400 aboveground communities with apartment-style complexes reached monumental proportions. Hundreds of rooms, built on several stories, clustered around plazas. Entire pueblos were built, along with trails connecting them to other pueblos. An enormous web of trade routes evolved.

The indigenous peoples, or Ancient Ones, as they were

ABOVE: ON A HIGH RIDGE OF ROCK IN NEW MEXICO'S BANDELIER NATIONAL MONUMENT, ON THE PAJARITO PLATEAU, IS CEREMONIAL CAVE, WHERE A KIVA OVERLOOKS THE CANYON BELOW. FIRST OCCUPIED BY THE ANASAZI IN THE LATE TWELFTH CENTURY, THE PLATEAU WAS ABANDONED IN THE EARLY SIXTEENTH CENTURY.

LEFT: BUILT OF STONES AND WITH A TIMBER ROOF, A NAVAJO HOGAN COVERED WITH EARTH STANDS AT THE BOTTOM OF ARIZONA'S CANYON DE CHELLY, ORIGINALLY AN ANCIENT ANASAZI SITE. NAVAJO AND ANASAZI ROCK ART IS VISIBLE ON THE CANYON WALLS.

later called by the Navajo who discovered traces of their existence, included the Hohokam in southern Arizona, the Anasazi in the Four Corners region, the Mogollon that occupied the mountainous regions straddling Arizona and New Mexico, the Sinagua located in north-central Arizona, plus numerous outlying groups. During the peak of development, a vast migration swept the region, believed to be caused by drought and persistent raids from other nomadic tribes. Each group abandoned its home and fields, leaving behind tools and architecture. Entire villages moved on to more defendable or well-watered locations. High on mesa tops or cliffs, they built with native rock and mud mortar, sometimes under south-facing overhangs that would collect the warm winter sun and shield the structures from the intense summer heat. Others moved to places with more reliable water sources, building from puddled earth or stone, leaving behind an architectural legacy that helped shape the future of desert architecture in the Southwest.

HOPI

LEFT: SET ON TOP OF THIRD
MESA IS ORAIBI, CONSIDERED
ONE OF THE OLDEST CONTINU-
OUSLY INHABITED VILLAGES IN
THE UNITED STATES. THE
HOUSES, OFTEN MULTISTORIED,
ARE CONSTRUCTED WITH ADOBE
MORTAR LAID BETWEEN COURSES
OF SANDSTONE BLOCKS, AND
OFTEN PLASTERED WITH MUD.

RIGHT: THE TRADITIONAL
HOPI VILLAGE OF WALPI,
BARELY VISIBLE HERE ON AN
OUTCROPPING OF ROCK, IS ON
FIRST MESA.

At the southern end of Black Mesa in northeastern Arizona, in a rocky, isolated, well-protected place, three finger-like projections rise above the desert floor. Villages of some ten thousand Hopi top these rocky escarpments, where houses sometimes teeter on the very edge of a cliff.

The communal areas of the old villages are staggered with roof terraces and built around a central plaza where ceremonial dances take place. The houses are often oriented with their backs to the cold winter winds and their fronts to the warming sun; the stones of which they are made come from the mesas, forming a harmonious union of architecture and landscape.

At one time, as with most tribal events, much ceremony surrounded the construction of a new house. When a house was to be built, a town crier would make an announcement to the entire village. Friends and clan members would go in search of building materials, each bringing something back, such as dressed stones, timbers, or poles. Dimensions were marked off, and then a prayer offering was made: eagle feathers given by a Hopi priest were placed under a large rock at each corner of the proposed structure. The traditional Hopi house song was sung while an offering of herbs and food was sprinkled on the ground, outlining the house.

Both men and women participated in building the house, which was traditionally constructed out of sandstone blocks from the nearby mesas or materials recycled from abandoned houses and then laid in irregular courses. Men put the beams in place. The women did the plastering and applied roofing materials such as poles, reeds, brush, and layers of earth, which finished off the flat-roofed structure. Parapets kept the earth from washing away. A fireplace with a plastered chimney hood above the hearth was built in a corner of the room, and interior walls were plastered and then whitewashed to keep them light. When the house was complete, prayer feathers and food offerings were put among the rafters, and a celebration was held inside the house, a feast for everyone to enjoy.

Usually located near the plaza is the kiva. A sunken place made from native stones, a kiva symbolically is built into Mother Earth, the birthplace of man. A ladder rises through a hole in the roof, representing man's emergence from the underworld to this world. A small hole in the floor, the sipapu, symbolizes the umbilical cord leading from Mother Earth and the path of man's emergence from the underworld. The kiva is often rectangular; its corners are defined by the four directions, with the length on the east-west

axis. Inside are two floor levels that represent previous worlds of the Hopi; the eastern half is always higher than the west. During male initiation rites novices stand

TOP: RESTING ON THIS ISOLATED MESA TOP IS HOTEVILLA. BUILT MOSTLY WITH SANDSTONE BLOCKS, THE HOMES BLEND IN WITH THE SANDSTONE MESA.

MIDDLE: HOPI INDIANS GROW MANY VARIETIES OF CORN WITH THE WATER THAT SEEPS OUT OF THE MESA INTO THE SANDY WASHES BELOW. CENTRAL TO HOPI CULTURE, CORN IS USED IN MANY OF THEIR CEREMONIES.

BOTTOM: A HOPI FARMER ON THIRD MESA TENDS HIS CORNFIELD. HE WEEDS AND SINGS TO HIS CROPS, HOPING TO ENSURE A SUCCESSFUL SEASON.

ON THIRD MESA, HOTEVILLA IS ONE OF THE MORE TRADITIONAL HOPI VILLAGES. THERE IS NO ELECTRICITY OR WATER IN THE CENTER OF THE VILLAGE. MANY TRADITIONAL HOPI BELIEVE THAT IF WATER FROM THE TAP, RATHER THAN WATER FROM THE SPRING, IS USED, THE IMPORTANCE OF WATER WILL BE FORGOTTEN.

on the raised level while the priests stand below. In the center is a fire pit, symbolic of where every Hopi's life began.

Most ceremonies center on the crops, particularly corn, and the precious rains needed to make them grow. Cornmeal is an important part of many rituals, for the Hopi believe corn was created for man in the first world, and when that world was destroyed corn was again given to him in the second world, and again in the third world. When man had to choose, he chose the smallest ear of corn, the same as the ear given to him in the first world, like the small ears of teosinte, the original wild corn from the south, believed to be the mother of all other corn.

The crops are irrigated with the water that seeps out of Black Mesa into the sandy washes below, creating tiny springs that produce healthy ears of corn, beans, squash, and some fruit trees. When the corn is ripe, the ears are spread out on roof tops to dry or roasted over coals and eaten later. The Hopi understand the significance of water — there is very little, and their lives depend on it. They also understand the relationship between Mother Earth and man, the core of their beliefs. It is essential they build their dwellings in harmony with the land and live with respect for its needs.

ACOMA

LEFT: MISSION SAN ESTEBAN DEL REY IN NEW MEXICO WAS BUILT IN 1640 WITH INDIAN LABOR. TIMBERS WERE HAULED FROM THE MOUNTAINS THIRTY MILES AWAY. BELLS HOUSED IN THE TOWERS WERE PRESENTED TO THE PEOPLE OF ACOMA BY THE KING OF SPAIN.

RIGHT: A DOUBLE LADDER AT THE ACOMA PUEBLO LEADS TO THE ENTRANCE OF A RECTANGULAR KIVA SET INTO A HOUSE COMPLEX.

Amid a forest of sandstone columns in western New Mexico is a sheared-off mesa rising nearly four hundred feet. It ends abruptly in a flat plain topped by the irregular surfaces of the multistoried pueblo of Acoma, continuously occupied since A.D. 1100.

The top of the mesa covers approximately seventy acres. A recently constructed road, flanked by carefully balanced rock pedestals, provides access to the top. Before the road was built, the only way up was by a stairway carved and hollowed out of the steep hillside, with handholds chiseled into the cliffs. This stairway is still actively used by the people of Acoma and a few of the more adventuresome tourists and visitors.

The village as a whole mirrors the surrounding mesas and is somewhat indiscernible from a distance. Terraced stone and adobe houses on well-organized streets occasionally are finished with a coat of mud or cement stucco. Often new houses will be attached to the top of existing ones, after permission has been obtained from the owner of the house below. Each of the stepped-back levels faces southward, maximizing exposure to the sun, while the long, continuous north walls shelter the apartment blocks from the cold northern winds. Lively colors painted on wooden window trim break up the repetitive patterns and long

straight lines and help distinguish individual houses. Wooden ladders furnish access to upper stories. Double ladders signify the entrance to a kiva. The rectangular kivas are believed to have been incorporated into the compounds in order to conceal them from Spanish missionaries, who, starting in the seventeenth century, were trying to convert every native they encountered.

In the main plaza is the Mission San Esteban del Rey. It was completed with the help of Indian labor in 1640 under the supervision of Fray Juan Ramirez. The earth and long timbers had to be carried from the valley below or from the distant mountainsides. The exterior facade is adorned with two bell towers — the bells were a gift presented to the people of Acoma from the king of Spain.

In front of the church is a large square plaza. The interior of the church measures 60 feet in width and 120 feet in length and boasts hand-carved corbels supporting wood vigas, or round beams, from nearby Mount Taylor. The main altar is separated into sections by spiral columns. Paintings and hand-carved sculptures decorate the spaces between the columns, and the altar railings are painted a vivid shade of pink, with turquoise highlights. The floor is earth.

In the attached convent, subtle designs decorate windows and small door openings that lead through long, cool passages. The exterior has a large bulbous buttress in the northeast corner and a recessed balcony with a brightly painted pink railing. The walls are massive, with soft, flowing edges that add to the church's majestic profile.

North of the main plaza, in the sandstone floor of the mesa, is a natural cistern. Augmented by springs, it provides water for the basic needs of the village throughout the winter months. Water is at a premium and often scarce, which is the main reason that only thirteen families live on the mesa year-round. Smaller, man-made cisterns are carved in rocks near house entrances, but supply only small quantities for immediate needs.

HIGH NORTHERN WALLS MADE FROM ADOBE AND STONE SHIELD ROW HOUSES FROM THE WINTER WINDS. TERRACED STORIES WITH SMALL PATIOS FACE THE SOUTH.

The gift of rain is summoned in many ways that are not always apparent to the outsider. During planting season, Acoma potters decorate their pots with finely painted lines, using black and white pigments symbolic of rain and clouds. Orange pigments signify the warmth and color connected with sunrise and sunset. Seeds are stored in pots with small openings in the center until the rains come. Then they are scattered around the fields by either shaking the seeds out or breaking the pot open.

There has never been electricity in Acoma. In addition to the sun, and aided by the insulation of massive exterior walls, fire-places are used as a source of heat in the winter. Kerosene lanterns are used for light. Much of the cooking, including the baking of breads, turnovers, and other baked goods, is done in outdoor beehive ovens called *hornos,* introduced by the Spanish.

With the exception of one or two new slump-block and concrete-block houses, the people of Acoma seem intent on keeping the village in its original condition as it gains significance today as a religious center. The ancient village, known as Sky City by the tourist industry, is a vital source of business for the Acoma tribe. Most important, it is an architectural treasure and a vital link with the past.

Named Sky City in tourist guidebooks, Acoma Pueblo sits on top of a seventy-acre chunk of sandstone that rises 367 feet in the air. On top, multistoried housing complexes are organized on an east-west axis with stepped-back levels that take advantage of a southern exposure.

TAOS PUEBLO

LEFT: IN THE HIGH DESERT OF NORTHERN NEW MEXICO, IT OFTEN SNOWS IN THE WINTER MONTHS. FIREPLACES ARE THE ONLY SOURCE OF HEAT. THERE IS NO ELECTRICITY OR RUNNING WATER IN THE ORIGINAL WALLED PART OF THE TAOS PUEBLO.

RIGHT: PUEBLO RESIDENTS ARE LAUNCHING ACTIVE PRESERVATION EFFORTS. ERODING WALLS ARE BEING REBUILT WITH NEW ADOBES, CUSTOM DOORS AND WINDOWS WHOSE DESIGNS ARE COMPATIBLE WITH THE ARCHITECTURE ARE REPLACING OLD ONES, AND DAMAGED ROOFS ARE UNDERGOING REPAIR.

In 1540, Hernando de Alvarado and a party of twenty men set out under orders from Coronado to explore the region to the east and north of the Zuni Pueblo in present-day New Mexico. Once reaching the Rio Grande valley they continued traveling north until arriving at what is now known as the Taos Pueblo in northern New Mexico. There they found two large communal houses terraced four and five stories high constructed from puddled adobe and covered with several coats of mud plaster. Access to the interior was by means of a ladder that led up to a flat roof where a smoke hole also served as an entrance by means of a second ladder. Inside was an open-hearth fire pit and a mud floor. A small fire using cedar or other woods with little pitch was kept continually burning to eliminate the irritating smoke that would be caused from the initial combustion. Roof terraces were used to expand living spaces, and as the need arose one cubicle was added on to the next.

Through the centuries only small changes have been made to the architecture of Taos Pueblo. Doors, windows, and freestanding houses have been added, and interior fireplaces with chimneys have eased the problem of smoke-filled rooms and blackened walls and ceilings. The pueblo is constantly renovated and maintained by the residents and by a preservation project run by them.

Two recent restoration innovations have been introduced by Joe Martinez, the current director of the preservation project. The once-unstable rooftops are being stabilized by using crusher finds from a gravel pit. The weight holds down the soil until the compaction creates a stabilized surface. The idea was formulated by Martinez while studying an anthill during a rainstorm. He discovered that the small gravel bits lining the outside of the ants' mound helped stabilize the entry. To help stabilize adobe, Martinez developed a method of shredding the straw used in adobe blocks and plaster in order to avoid the perils of straw's tubular stems. The long hollow tubes often provide homes for insect larvae and create passageways for rainwater to enter the core of the adobe. Shredding the straw eliminates both problems. When used in the plaster mix, shredded straw won't hold the moisture that can freeze in the winter and cause the plaster to pop off the walls.

Even though the new wall sections in the pueblo use adobe bricks and mud plaster, they cannot be differentiated visually from the old, puddled-adobe walls. Walls of the pueblo are a natural, comfortable brown, soft and uneven, wavering in places before straightening out for another few feet. Yearly

TOP: A CREW, WORKING UNDER THE GUIDANCE OF PRESERVATION DIRECTOR JOE MARTINEZ, PLASTERS A WALL AT THE TAOS PUEBLO WITH A MIXTURE OF ADOBE MUD AND SHREDDED STRAW. MARTINEZ OBSERVES: "IN A WOOD FRAME HOUSE THERE ARE A LOT OF CRACKS. I CAN HEAR THE WIND WHISTLING, AND WORRY THE HOUSE MIGHT BLOW AWAY. AND IT'S NOISY. I CAN HEAR ECHOES WHICH ARE NOT A PART OF ME. BUT IN AN ADOBE HOME I CAN FEEL MY HEARTBEAT BECAUSE THE HOUSE HAS BECOME ONE WITH ME. WHEN I'M INSIDE, THE WALLS BREATHE WITH ME AND THERE'S A SOFTNESS TO IT. ADOBE ABSORBS SOUND. IT LISTENS SO I CAN THINK. IN THE WINTER I LIGHT A FIRE IN THE FIREPLACE, SIT DOWN, RELAX, AND IN FIVE MINUTES I'M AT PEACE AND GO TO SLEEP."

BOTTOM: MUD PLASTER COVERS THE EXTERIOR WALLS AT THE TAOS PUEBLO. INHABITED FOR MORE THAN ONE THOUSAND YEARS, THE COMPOUND IS THE LARGEST MULTISTORIED ADOBE COMPLEX IN NORTH AMERICA TO BE CONTINUOUSLY INHABITED.

wall maintenance is a necessary group project. Traditionally, the men of the pueblo perform the heaviest work, mixing and carrying loads of mud to the site, while the women plaster the exterior walls, throwing on mud with their hands and spreading it around with their fingers before finishing the surface with a small, pointed trowel. In recent years Martinez and a number of pueblo laborers have taken over some of the traditional plastering in order to try out different techniques that may add to the longevity of the pueblo. The preservation crew is also replacing the old canales, or roof drains, with a wider design lined with sheet metal and tapered at the end. Residents are encouraged to practice active maintenance, including regular snow removal from their flat roofs. Some of the owners cooperate, but others, who are elderly or not year-round residents, have let their sections go.

Taos Pueblo is the oldest pueblo made of adobe in North America that is still inhabited. The people do not have electricity, running water, or indoor plumbing, but the residents of Taos Pueblo feel they have what they need. Taos Creek, which flows year-round through the central plaza, provides fresh water, and kerosene lanterns and fireplaces supply sufficient light and heat.

MAYO

LEFT: THE RIBS FROM THE PITAHAYA OR ORGAN-PIPE CACTUS ARE WOVEN BETWEEN *HORCÓNES,* OR FORKED SUPPORTS. MUD FROM THE BANKS OF THE RIVER FILLS IN BETWEEN THE RIBS AND IS USED FOR INTERIOR AND EXTERIOR PLASTER.

RIGHT: MAYO INDIANS, NOTED FOR THEIR FINE CRAFTSMANSHIP, USE NATURAL FIBERS AND DYES IN THEIR RUGS AND WOOD FROM LOCAL TREES FOR THEIR WOODEN MASKS.

The land around Teachibe, a Mayo Indian village in southern Sonora, Mexico, is broad and level, with crisscrossing drainageways and large arroyos. In the summer the heat builds until the clouds move across the sky with heavy loads of moisture, gathering up enough force to extinguish the bright light of the sun and generate a gentle wind. Within minutes the heavens open up, unleashing their fury on the land, turning dry arroyos into raging rivers, and flooding areas with sheets of running water that etch deep lines into the earth. The storm may last an hour or only a few minutes; soft slow rains are uncommon.

The earth is generally dusty and brown, with thorny trees, shrubs, and cacti dominating the landscape. Large mesquite trees cluster around arroyos, stretching their roots as much as 150 feet downward for water. The pods produced by the mesquite are harvested by the Indians and ground into flour, which is used to bake breads and other foods.

Tall prickly pear cacti can be found growing next to fences made from skeletons of organ-pipe cacti or cultivated in fields as a crop to harvest. The pads of the prickly pear, called *nopales,* are cooked and eaten as a delicacy throughout Mexico and parts of the American Southwest. Many desert plants are vital to the lives of the Mayo, especially those used for medicinal purposes. As young

THE PORTAL ON A MAYO HOME IN TEACHIBE USUALLY FACES EAST TOWARD THE RISING SUN. DURING THE HEAT OF THE DAY, THIS PORCH KEEPS THE MAIN LIVING AREA IN SHADE.

children, the Mayo learn about the special properties of the plants unique to their environment.

Most of the families in the area grow squash, beans, and corn by the banks of the arroyo where the water, when running, can easily be diverted for irrigation. The Mayo plant their crops by the full moon in the belief that they will not fail. The cycle of the moon also influences when houses are built in Teachibe. Wood for building is always cut during certain cycles of the moon. When there is a new moon, the Mayo believe the wood will be vulnerable to the damaging effects of insects.

In the center of the village of Teachibe the Moroyoqui family lives in a typical sculpted house of pitahaya ribs gathered from the organ-pipe cactus. The ribs, which are woven between mesquite supports, are filled and plastered with earth from the nearby banks of the river. Vigas span the width of the house and protrude from the tops of walls, forming a natural framework for the roof. Between the vigas, pitahaya ribs are set close together with a layer of brush from the sitavaro plant. A thick layer of fine-particle soil added to the roof sheds moisture and caps and seals the structure from the weather. The family, which has always lived in Teachibe, has occupied this house for thirty-five years.

Attached to the east side of the Moroyoqui house is a portal, held up by forked supports called *horcónes*. Like all porches in the village, it opens to the east.

TOP: ADOBE BRICKS ARE COVERED WITH A LAYER OF GRASS WEIGHTED DOWN BY MORE ADOBES TO PROTECT THEM FROM THE SUMMER RAINS.

BOTTOM: *NOPALES* GROW OVER A FENCE IN MASIACA, A MAYO VILLAGE IN SOUTHERN SONORA, MEXICO. THE PADS ARE COOKED AND EATEN AS A DELICACY IN MEXICO AND PARTS OF THE SOUTHWEST.

Jesus Jose Nieblas, who lives down the road in an old adobe and is a relative of the Moroyoquis, tells of the Mayo philosophy for desert living: "In the morning, when the sun comes up, it is a gentle warming sun that comes under the portal. By the time the sun has gained strength, it is overhead and screened from the house. And by afternoon, in the heat of the day, the east side where you live is in the shade and [the sun] casts long shadows."

In the hot summer months the Moroyoqui family lives and sleeps outside under the protection of their covered portal, which functions not only as a porch, but as an outdoor living room as well. When the evening temperatures take a significant drop in the winter, the household withdraws into a small interior room and closes the doors, maintaining warmth by the insulation provided by the earth on the roof and walls. Small window openings let in only a minimal amount of hot or cold air. Jesus Jose Nieblas firmly believes in the insulating properties of walls made with earth — "They are never too cold or too hot" — and he warns against the use of concrete. "Concrete will always be cold when it's cold, and hot when it's hot. It is not a good material to build houses from."

NORTHERN MEXICO

Although northern Mexico has a diversified landscape, most of the region is linked together by the common thread of aridity. The vast desert terrain, which is bisected by mountain ranges and outlined with coastal plains, reflects the dryness in its cracked and rocky soils that support only specially adapted plants and animals.

In the extreme northwest lies Baja California, an eight-hundred-mile peninsula separated from the mainland by the Gulf of California. A mountainous spine runs down its length, splitting the east side from the west, or the Pacific Ocean from the Gulf. Most of Baja is made up of subdivisions of the Sonoran Desert, which include dry lakes, deserts, mountains, canyons, and coastlines with early morning fog.

Howling winds blow across the Pacific coast, continually eroding and changing the shape of the shoreline. Dunes shift and grow, moving farther inland. This is a land where the rainfall varies from little to none, and where hot springs can be found bubbling out of the earth near the base of the mountains, staining the soils ocher and sienna.

The plants are also unique; many are inhospitable, with daggerlike spines. Some are endemic. Others are so strange-looking they appear unearthly. There are cirios, or *Idria columinaris*, odd-shaped plants thought to be related to the ocotillo that resemble huge carrots turned upside down. Giant barrel cacti lean over cliffsides, producing brilliant-colored flowers. Agaves come in many varieties, growing from coastal areas to steep hillsides.

At one time the Indian population of Baja numbered in the ten thousands. Today there are approximately five hundred Indians left. They were wiped out by disease brought to them by the colonizing Spaniards. The remaining Pai Pai and Kumiai live in adobe villages not far from the northern border, where they make pottery and weave baskets from natural materials. The rest of Baja is a patchwork of cities, old missions, agricultural communities, and new resorts, with large undeveloped areas in between.

Sonora is in the northwest portion of mainland Mexico and contains a large section of the Sonoran Desert and a part of the Sinaloan thorn forest, a transitional area believed to be the origin of the Sonoran Desert. There are flat grasslands with mesquite trees, acacias and tall cacti, and soft slopes leading to steep hillsides covered in thorny shrub. In the hillside canyons, exotic fig trees and smooth-skinned octopus agaves grow. The agaves cling precariously to the side of the canyon cliff, with their roots wedged into cracks in the rocks. This land changes seasonally. A metamorphosis occurs between June and July, the time between drought and thunderstorm.

Yaqui, Mayo, and Seri Indian villages are scattered about the countryside. Their houses make use of the earth and local plants. Trees provide posts and beams, cacti skeletons are woven together for wall sections, brush is used on rooftops, and a slurry of mud covers the framework.

The historic towns of Spanish Colonial houses built around

PRECEDING PAGES: The morning sun pours through the windows of the bell tower of Bishop Reyes Cathedral in Alamos, Sonora. The stone cathedral dates back to 1803.

BELOW: Hacienda San Diego is one of the seven haciendas in Chihuahua built for Luís Terrazas in 1902. Cast-iron columns and stone pillars support the portal that wraps around three sides of the house.

ABOVE: THE COTTON HOME IN ALAMOS, SONORA, HAS OUTDOOR DINING AND SITTING ROOMS. ALL OF THE ROOMS OPEN ONTO A PORTAL THAT IS CONSTRUCTED WITH WOODEN BEAMS. A LARGE COURTYARD IS IN THE CENTER.

RIGHT: THE CASA DEL OBISPO, OR BISHOP'S HOUSE, IN ALAMOS HAS TWO STORIES, WITH IRON GRILLWORK COVERING THE DOORS AND WINDOWS. BEAUTIFULLY CARVED STONEWORK SURROUNDS A PAIR OF SPANISH COLONIAL DOORS ON THE FRONT ENTRANCE.

town plazas date from the 1700s and 1800s. Their architecture was brought over from Spain, with roots traceable to North Africa. Covered porches and courtyards provide expanded living areas. Ceilings are high and openings minimal. Insulation from the heat and cold is provided by the thick walls of adobe bricks.

In the state of Chihuahua, in northeastern Mexico, summer flash floods bring torrents of water out of the mountains, down the bajadas, and across the desert plains, creating gashlike drainages that crisscross the high desert. Located between two mountain ranges, the Sierra Madre Occidental on the west and the Sierra Madre Oriental on the east, the Chihuahuan Desert is characterized by the creosote bush, a drought-resistant shrub with medicinal properties. A wide variety of other plants thrive in the gypsum and limestone soils, including tarbush, acacia, mesquite, ocotillo, yucca, agave, and cacti. The last-known wild Mexican gray wolf was captured in this region. Bighorn and pronghorn still roam in limited numbers.

It was in this dry, desolate land of hot summers and cold winters that Apache drove out Mexican colonists who dared to stay any length of time. Fear of the Apache helped men like Luís Terrazas to become one of the largest landowners in the country during the nineteenth century. People were eager to sell their property, sometimes for ten cents an acre, and Terrazas was smart enough to buy, until he accumulated fifteen million acres, seven haciendas, and four hundred thousand head of cattle by the end of the century.

Sprawling haciendas were owned by few and run by many.

Encircled by high walls, they usually were built on a knoll. The main house centered on a courtyard with plastered adobe walls and stone corners and columns. Large beams were transported from the Sierras for roof supports. Lumber was milled on the site and used to build doors, shutters, and furniture.

After the revolution in Chihuahua, the state began rebuilding under the direction of President Obregón in 1920. He opened lands for settlement to various sects, including groups of Mormons and Mennonites, that would turn the region into productive farmland.

Today, the industrious people of Chihuahua have used the desert to their advantage, growing food crops, raising livestock, mining gold and silver, and building a new architecture around the old.

ALAMOS
HACIENDA

In the southern portion of Sonora, not far from the Gulf of California, the town of Alamos lies nestled in the foothills at the base of the Sierra Madre. Alamos was once the silver-mining capital of northern Mexico, prospering throughout the eighteenth century until, during the nineteenth and early twentieth centuries, Yaqui Indian raids helped to reduce the local population. By the beginning of the twentieth century, only two thousand residents remained in the battle-scarred town.

The restoration and rebirth of Alamos began in the mid-1900s, and today the town is an architectural treasure. As with most towns in Mexico, Alamos is laid out in con-

ventional squares surrounding plazas. One house on the main plaza, next to the cathedral, is a Spanish Colonial hacienda that originally was the home of Chato Almada, the son of Don Jose Maria Almada, one of the town's most prominent residents in the early 1800s.

Herrick and Elizabeth Nuzum purchased the house in 1969. Their dream house had not been lived in for more than fifty years, and it had last been used as a carpenter's shop. There were still wood shavings on the floor, and the house was essentially a ruin, albeit a historical one.

Originally the house had been two blocks long and divided into three sections, each with a center patio or courtyard. The Nuzums purchased the first two sections and started the process of joining them together again, which took five years.

Outside the entrance to the house is a covered walkway with pillars of *cantera*, a soft stone that can be found in the hills around Alamos. Plaster once covered the pillars, but when Elizabeth Nuzum discovered the beautiful stonework underneath, she had the plaster removed. Behind the pillars are two grand wooden panel doors, with a smaller door cut into one, opening onto a spacious zaguan, leading to the front, or main, courtyard.

The rooms of the first section are large with high beamed ceilings and massive adobe walls that open onto the central court-

yard. The street side has high windows with solid panel shutters that close out the heat of the day and the noise and dust of the town.

The Nuzums wanted to keep the house as simple as possible without disturbing its

TOP: MASKS FROM THE NEARBY YAQUI AND MAYO INDIANS COVER ONE WALL OF THE COLLECTIONS ROOM. ON AN ADJACENT WALL, A KEYHOLE WINDOW, RECALLING A SHAPE SEEN EXTENSIVELY IN NORTH AFRICA, LETS IN MORNING SUNLIGHT.

BOTTOM: COVERED PORCHES AND SITTING AREAS SURROUND THE FRONT COURTYARD ON THREE SIDES.

A LARGE KITCHEN WITH A CENTER ISLAND HAS AN INTIMATE BREAKFAST AREA WITH *EQUIPALE,* OR MEXICAN PIGSKIN FURNITURE, AND A VIEW OUT ONTO THE MIDDLE PATIO. LOW-FIRE TILES FROM JALISCO, MEXICO, FRAME THE INTERIOR WINDOW.

integrity or regional flavor. The house, with numerous courtyards and gardens, is designed for outdoor living. The main courtyard has the most formal garden. In one corner an old olive tree reaches up with gnarled branches and shades this portion of the house from the midday sun. The covered portal runs the length of three sides of the courtyard with several seating areas.

The three other gardens include a roof garden, which is the Nuzums' private sanc-

tuary, providing wonderful views of the town and surrounding hillsides; a Japanese garden; and a back courtyard with a small pool and a garden filled with colorful vines and flowers.

In the Japanese garden, a rock wall with wild orchids rooted in its cracks connects the first section of the house to the second. A pair of small antique doors, set into the middle of the wall, leads to a special-collections room, where Herrick Nuzum

LUNCHES AND DINNERS ARE
OFTEN SERVED IN THE OUTDOOR
DINING AREA. A CARVED STONE
CHIMENEA, OR FIREPLACE, FROM
GUANAJUATO PROVIDES HEAT
ON COOLER DAYS.

displays unusual pieces such as old coins and Yaqui Indian masks. This section of the house also includes two guest bedrooms and Elizabeth Nuzum's sewing workroom located off the back courtyard.

The house had no fireplaces, but the Nuzums remedied that by building fireplaces in most of the rooms. Even the outdoor dining area has an elaborate stone-carved fireplace Elizabeth Nuzum found in Guanajuato. While most of the fireplaces are not used on a daily basis, when the temperature drops in rare cold weather the house is closed up and fires are lit in the

THE GARDEN IN THE FRONT COURTYARD BLOOMS IN ALL WHITE. IN THE CENTER, WATER BUBBLES FROM A STONE FOUNTAIN FILLED WITH KOI FISH, IMPORTED FROM JAPAN, AND FLOATING LILIES. BREEZES BLOWING ACROSS THE WATER PRODUCE A SLIGHT COOLING EFFECT. THE PATIO IS PAVED WITH LOW-FIRE ADOBES FROM A NEARBY SOURCE.

main living areas — the kitchen and master bedroom.

Warm weather in this region is generally more of a problem than cold. Window shutters can be closed during the heat of the day, and ceiling fans circulate the air. The Nuzums were surprised to discover that the opening over the front door also provides vital cross-ventilation. In the summer when it's extremely hot, afternoon breezes move through the house and out the opening. It's a house that breathes naturally and works easily within the confines of its environment.

MENNONITES OF CHIHUAHUA

In the 1920s, Chihuahua, under the leadership of President Obregón, agreed not only to sell land to the Mennonites, but to release them from the usual government controls. Today, there are more than thirty-five thousand Mennonites living in colonies throughout Chihuahua.

Many factions of Mennonites have split off from one another over the years — some are more conservative, while others want electricity and pickup trucks or more mechanized farm equipment. But their basic beliefs in hard work and the Bible are the same, as is their style of architecture.

North of Casas Grandes in Chihuahua, just east of the Corralitos River where irri-

gation has changed the desert to fertile fields, lies the village of Campo Capulin, where Abraham Wiebe lives with his wife and children. In keeping with the conservative views of the residents, there is no electricity in the houses at Campo Capulin, nor are there motorized cars.

Like other Mennonites in the area, Abraham Wiebe considered the harsh desert environment carefully and built a house that worked with the climate as well as provided for his family's spiritual needs. By using adobe bricks mixed with straw, and mud for mortar, his house in effect grew out of the soil on his land. A pitched roof of corrugated sheet metal helps keep the house cool by

reflecting the sun's intense rays. Similar to the dwellings of the Mayo Indians in Sonora, the house is oriented to the east to catch only the morning sun. The front entrance, which is also a breezeway, provides shade during most of the day, especially during long, hot summers.

Along the back, or west, side of the house, a row of four cottonwood trees offers shade in summer, but allows exposure to the sun in winter when the leaves are shed. A willow and a chinaberry tree protect the north, and an overhang shades the entry to the south, where three wood-sash windows

catch the winter sun. Large gardens, tended by the women of the family, are in the front and to the side, ringed by native plants, including the Mexican bird-of-paradise. Grapevines, peanuts, watermelon, cucumbers, carrots, tomatoes, and corn provide fresh food most of the year, supplemented by home-canned vegetables.

The interior of the house reflects the plain and simple philosophy of the people who live in it. Two wings are connected by the central breezeway. The kitchen and dining rooms are in the north wing, and the bedrooms to the south. The kitchen is a long

VINES COVER THE FRONT ENTRY, WHICH CONNECTS THE TWO SIDES OF THE HOUSE AND FACES EAST, TOWARD THE MORNING SUN. COLORFUL FLOWERS ARE MIXED IN WITH THE VEGETABLE GARDEN.

rectangular room in which one end is for cooking and the other for sitting and eating. A banjo-style windup wall clock is in one corner by a long straight-backed wooden bench and table. Across from the table, against the opposite wall, four chairs sit on the highly polished linoleum floor.

The bedrooms have ample room to ac-commodate more beds as the need arises. Muslin window coverings are neatly folded over to let the light enter. Behind the curtains are plain white shades that can be lowered during the heat of the day or lifted to allow the sunlight to penetrate, depending on the season.

There is a soothing silence that echoes throughout the house, and even though it's sparsely furnished, the materials and colors exude a warmth and an openness that give a comfortable feeling. One can understand why the younger generation continues to practice the traditions of its elders.

RANCHO CORRALITOS

I n northeastern Mexico, miles and miles of fenced land are filled with creosote bushes, acacias, and scrubby mesquites. Dust devils spin wide circles of churned-up earth, leaving behind a fine covering of silt. Only the rains help to cleanse the land and release the fresh smells from the creosote bush.

The Corralitos River winds its way through this region, a narrow watercourse that makes the eastern valley bloom with green fields of high corn, sunflowers, and other food crops. Stout cottonwoods line the riverbanks, bending their trunks precariously over the edge of the banks, toppling down when the soil becomes too wet to hold on to the roots. Piles of plant debris and deadwood are stacked along the river, indicative of the occasional overflow onto the surrounding lowlands.

Amid white-faced cattle roaming the desert scrub is a wood board, with a brand burned into it, hanging between two fence posts. This is the entrance to Rancho Corralitos, once the second-largest cattle operation in Mexico, with more than a million acres of land.

Originally a Spanish land grant, Corralitos at one time supported forty thousand head of cattle, twenty thousand sheep, fifteen hundred people, a railroad, and a smelter. It also had several productive mines,

yielding gold, silver, copper, and lead. Around the turn of the century, at the time when Porfirio Diaz was opening Mexico's doors to foreign investors, J. P. Morgan interests purchased the ranch. However, the Mexican revolution interfered with profits, and by 1912 Corralitos had sustained losses of more than one million dollars from property damage and cattle and horse thefts. Eventually the property was sold and resold until it landed in the hands of Bill Wallace, who currently lives at the ranch headquarters with his wife, Imelda, and four children.

The Wallace family has ties to the land dating as far back as 1885, when Bill Wallace's grandfather, William Wallace, left his family in Ohio at age seventeen to work for the Corralitos Cattle and Mining operation. He worked and lived on the ranch until his death in 1905. During the revolution, Bill's father, William Walter Wallace, left the ranch to live in El Paso and did not return until 1939, when he was hired as a mule skinner. Over a period of time, he won the friendship of his employer, General Rodrigo Quevedo, who eventually agreed to sell him the ranch headquarters at a bargain price.

Today, time and neglect have reduced

THE FAMILY CHAPEL IS AN ADOBE BUILDING THAT HAS BEEN RECENTLY RESTORED BY THE PRESENT OWNERS, BILL AND IMELDA WALLACE. THE RUST COLOR THAT STAINS THE OUTSIDE WALLS IS FROM THE EARTH PILED ON THE ROOF THAT WASHES OUT THE CANALES.

many of the original buildings to crumbling walls of adobe or scattered mounds of rubble, but the main compound is still intact, surrounded by high rambling walls and broad-canopied shade trees. Originally a hacienda, Corralitos still possesses much of the ambience of its earlier history. The compound divides into two sections. The north section of the house remains a simple room-to-room U-shaped layout opening onto a central courtyard. Many rooms have twelve-foot high ceilings with viga roof supports and split-cedar stakes running crosswise in a herringbone pattern. Eighteen inches of

claylike soil on the top of roof is covered with a layer of cement. Wall widths range from three to six feet. The irregular wall surfaces are coated with plaster and painted white. Most of the floors are scored colored concrete or wood planks. Originally the window openings throughout the house were small square holes cut into the adobe walls and covered by iron bars for security. These were later replaced by steel-sash windows, many of which look out over a vast expanse of grassland and cottonwood trees.

Usually doors and windows are left open to catch the breezes and help cross-venti-

late the interior. The thick adobe walls and ceilings keep room temperatures stable throughout the day and night. The open end of the U faces east, with the central portion shaded by the portal, letting in early morning sun and creating shade in the afternoon when the heat intensifies. A large droopy willow provides shade at one end of the courtyard garden.

The large, square kitchen, located on one end of the U, is where most of the ranch activity takes place. Against one wall are both a woodstove and a gas stove and a large vintage refrigerator. Lining the other wall is a sink with ample counter space on each side and pine cabinets that frame a large window. A covered breezeway next to the kitchen leads to a storage area with a freezer, an extra refrigerator, and shelves full of canned goods.

Beyond the kitchen is one of two formal dining rooms in the compound; this one is the smaller of the two, with seating for eight. Above the corner fireplace, used in the winter during brief periods when the temperature drops, hang antique branding irons, spurs, and old bridle pieces that record the earlier years at Corralitos.

AN ELEGANT DINING ROOM WITH MAHOGANY WAINSCOTING AND WOOD-FRONT VENEER ON THE FIREPLACE SEATS TWENTY PEOPLE.

The substantial living room is typical of a working ranch — filled with comfortable overstuffed furniture and end tables with wagon-wheel designs cut in their bases. Ancient Indian pottery decorates the mantel of a large, square fireplace. Other Indian artifacts are scattered around the room, including framed arrowhead collections, metates and manos, or grinding stones, and stone hatchets and hammerheads, which were found embedded in the soil or simply lying around the property.

The southern section of the compound is constructed in a traditional square enclosing a courtyard that can be entered through arched openings at either end. During the last several years, the Wallace family has renovated a number of rooms in this section. The formal dining room has paneled mahogany wainscoting that matches the wood-front veneer on the fireplace. An adjacent room that functions as an intimate bar has split varnished logs aligning the walls halfway up, creating a built-in bench. Cow skulls hang on the wall, and family photos decorate the corner fireplace. Both rooms have entries to the courtyard, where sidewalks and grass provide for outdoor living.

The house is old and in need of constant maintenance. The Wallaces are slowly restoring and remodeling one room at a time.

While they restore the square section, they are living in the U-shaped segment of the house. Bill Wallace concedes that it would be more prudent to build a new house and believes the daily need for patching and fixing is why many old adobe buildings are allowed to melt away. Nevertheless, the Wallace family will continue to patch, fix, and restore Corralitos, as previous generations did before them.

The entire compound has an elegance that can only come from a time when the affluent flourished in this part of the world. Each hacienda had its own staff of carpenters, blacksmiths, saddle makers, and weavers and an area to accommodate their trades. There were buildings where cattle and sheep were butchered, and warehouses to store meat, hides, wool, and grain. Religious needs were met by a chapel on the property, next to the main house. The hacienda was a self-sustaining compound that was often run and owned by a single family. Corralitos is a living memory of an era gone by.

BAJA CLIFF HOUSE

LEFT: A LONG PORCH FACING
THE OCEAN RUNS ALONG THE
WEST SIDE OF THE BAJA CLIFF
HOUSE. BRUCE EICHER
DESIGNED THE OUTDOOR
FURNISHINGS.

RIGHT: A FOURTEENTH-CENTURY
STONE ARCHANGEL FROM
GUANAJUATO, MEXICO,
STANDS GUARD IN THE ENTRY
COURTYARD.

N ear the town of La Misión, on the Pacific coast in Baja California, steep cliffs end abruptly at the water's edge. This area of Baja is considered a coastal desert, characterized by infrequent rains and early-morning fog. Clusters of coastal agaves and salt-tolerant plants thrive in the sandy soils. Short stretches of white beach contrast with dark, forbidding rocks. Houses are strung along the top of the cliff, overlooking the vast expanse of blue water and thundering surf. This location and the lure of Mexico drew Bruce Eicher, a lighting and furniture designer and manufacturer, south from California to his present home.

In 1977 Eicher spent several weekends at a friend's eight-hundred-square-foot house on the beach in La Misión, Baja. Several years later he discovered it was for sale, bought the property, and in effect started over again on a sheet of brown butcher paper, the birthplace of all Eicher's designs. He redesigned the house around a collection of artifacts he had amassed over the years — entire floors from Spanish Colonial haciendas and authentic colonial furnishings from Mexico, including antique doors. He hired stonemasons from central Mexico to lay the floors and set the columns, found tiles in the town of Dolores Hidalgo outside Guadalajara, and had glass for the windows trucked three times from California. Twice

the glass shattered before being installed.

Palms, bougainvillea, and trailing vines camouflage the front facade, making it difficult to tell if the house is new or centuries old. The design of the front of the house revolves around five pairs of three-hundred-year-old matching Colonial doors from Mexico that open at different elevations onto balconies with iron railings. Smooth-plastered walls are topped with a decorative cap that runs along the parapet, and protruding rams are carved out of stone to drain the rainwater away from the walls.

A pair of seventeenth-century doors cre-

ates a grand entrance to a stone-paved courtyard facing the Pacific Ocean. The house is perched on the edge of a rock cliff, with long views across the water to the western horizon; this view, coupled with the hypnotic sound of waves ceaselessly breaking against the rocks below, is an effective tranquilizer.

Flat stone slabs of varying sizes pave the patio and continue into the living room and out to the covered portales on the west side of the house. The living room is a lofty space with large windows and glass doors to the west. Sabino, a cypress wood from Mexico, frames the enormous doors that slide back, integrating the interior space with the outside. The living room stretches as wide as the dimensions of the property allow. The ceiling rises more than twenty feet and is spanned by square beams with plaster in between. An interior balcony runs across the south wall, looking down on the sitting area and the decorative stone carving on the fireplace. Primitive pieces mix easily with lights and furnishings designed by the owner.

The house takes breathtaking advantage of the site by opening up the spectacular western views with a series of patios that follows the natural elevations of the terrain and makes creative use of the designer's impressive collection of materials and furniture. In one bedroom there are patterned ceiling tiles between wooden beams, a free-standing round fireplace with a masonry hood, and a raised platform supporting a bed with an elaborately carved wooden head-board. Another bedroom has a metal four-poster bed with whimsical branches, twigs, and leaves topping each of the posts — a creation of the owner.

Outside, facing west, balconies are supported by Tarascan Indian columns from old log cabins that date back to the sixteenth century. Other decorative touches are authentic stone geodes formed by volcanic gases and primitive wood pieces among comfortable outdoor furniture, also creations by the owner.

The kitchen and eating area form a large open space with tile work patterned after a kiosk in the middle of Dolores Hidalgo. On the east wall an arched alcove is fronted by stone columns and covered inside with deco-

TOP: BETWEEN THE BEAMS IN THE MASTER SUITE ARE MEXICAN TILES, LAID OUT IN A CHEVRON PATTERN.

MIDDLE: A FIREPLACE AND WEST-FACING WINDOWS HEAT THE UPSTAIRS BEDROOM. THE ROOM OPENS UP TO A WEST PATIO THAT SKIRTS THE EDGE OF A CLIFF JUTTING ABOVE THE PACIFIC OCEAN.

BOTTOM: YELLOW, BLUE, AND WHITE TILES ARRANGED IN A UNIQUE PATTERN COVER THE CENTER ISLAND AND COUNTERS IN THE KITCHEN. THE INSPIRATION FOR THE DESIGN CAME FROM A MEXICAN KIOSK.

rative tile work. Above the center island hangs a lighting fixture with hooks for pots and pans that is a reproduction of a French meat rack, with fanciful creatures decorating the ironwork. A round table and chairs are in front of a fireplace with a carved stone mantel, a source of heat when the cool breezes blow off the ocean.

Cooling is simple. "It never gets that hot," explains Bruce Eicher, "and the house has natural ventilation if I open the doors on both sides and let the ocean breeze blow through." The ocean's moisture creates a primitive evaporative cooling system, which is large enough to be extremely effective.

During the building process many of the usual horror stories plagued the project, which is to be expected when building an unusual home with an often-absent owner. "The house was an enormous experience," relates Bruce Eicher. "Baja doesn't have any houses like this, so it was hard to find skilled labor in the right areas." Fortunately he found Raul Lujan, a very talented builder nearby who was able to take Eicher's ideas and translate them into what he envisioned. But Eicher concedes, "It takes enormous patience to do something like this." Enormous patience and a great sense of design — Bruce Eicher has both.

NEW MEXICO

ew Mexico, known as the Land of Enchantment, is also a land of extremes — geographically, climatically, and culturally.

In the north-central region, the southern Rockies spill over from Colorado, bringing with them a high-altitude plant community: Douglas fir, spruce, pine, and aspen. Rivers fed by mountain streams move through deep canyons as they make their way farther south. There, mesas give way to hills and exposed rock faces that are banded with the colors of New Mexico — yellow, buff, and deep red.

In the northwestern section of the state, the Colorado Plateau is broken up by flat mesas of rosy sandstone cut open by

deep ravines that continue to the broad valleys below. Piñon and juniper are mixed in with sagebrush and grasses.

To the east, the plains of Texas roll in, dotted with mesquite trees and covered by grasslands. Mountains appear in the distance.

To the south is the Chihuahuan Desert. Dagger-sharp yuccas with clusters of seasonal white blooms, resinous creosote bushes, and spiny prickly pear cacti all thrive in the harsh sun-

ABOVE: ON THE PLAZA IN LAS TRAMPAS IN NORTHERN NEW MEXICO IS THE CHURCH SAN JOSÉ DE GARCÍA. STANDING SINCE 1760, THE ADOBE HAS WALLS THIRTY-FOUR FEET HIGH AND FOUR FEET THICK AT THE BASE.

LEFT: THE CHURCH IN THE VILLAGE OF LA CUEVA HAS RECENTLY BEEN RESTORED. LOCATED ON THE EAST SIDE OF THE SANGRE DE CRISTO MOUNTAINS IN NORTHEASTERN NEW MEXICO, IT IS A SIMPLE ADOBE STRUCTURE WITH WOODEN GOTHIC-STYLE WINDOWS.

PRECEDING PAGES: SHIPROCK, A SACRED PLACE OF THE NAVAJO, IS A VOLCANIC PLUG IN NORTHWESTERN NEW MEXICO.

light of this high-desert floor.

Scattered in isolated pockets around the state are badlands with their fantasy-like forms, white gypsum sands, and folds of black lava. Skies flash shades of orange, red, and purple when the sun meets the horizon. Occasional light shows are highlighted by thunderstorms or periods of drought in the summer, and icy winds and snowcapped peaks in the winter.

The lack of water in New Mexico has caused a concentration of development along the watercourses, beginning in prehistoric times after ancient peoples crossed the Bering Straits from Asia and headed south. It is speculated that during the Ice Age, when the oceans were receding and creating landmasses, herds of animals began to migrate, moving on to richer grasslands. In turn, people followed in pursuit of game, eventually working their way to the Southwest. When the indigenous peoples learned a more agrarian lifestyle, communal settlements were established around the state, and by the time the Spaniards arrived, thriving pueblos were located on mesa tops and along river valleys.

In the early sixteenth century, Nuñez Cabeza de Vaca and his companions were the first Spaniards to set foot in present-day New Mexico. The embellished reports of a preliminary investigation by Fray Marcos de Niza encouraged the more extensive excursion by Coronado and his men in 1540. But it was not until the end of the sixteenth century that there was any serious effort to colonize New Mexico. At that time missionaries, soldiers, and families arrived and brought with them livestock, horses, and iron tools that helped shape the future of New Mexico.

A combination of architecture from Spain and that of the Indian pueblo communities was the basis for a regional style of design in the Southwest. Missions and colonies were built with the aid of wood forms to produce adobes, an iron ax and an adze to cut long roof timbers, and horses to haul the lumber from remote locations. Beams were squared off, and corbels were elaborately carved. The Spaniards built fireplaces with chimneys and kept outside openings minimal for the purpose of defense. A courtyard plan was used for both the self-contained hacienda and the town as a method of fortification. This was accomplished by building homes around a town plaza with secured entranceways. Large walls with few openings and flat roofs covered with earth insulated homes, creating a dark but comfortable environment.

In 1821, the same year Mexico achieved independence from Spain, the Santa Fe Trail opened the way for trappers, traders, and merchants from the east. Wagons brought milled lumber and supplies, plus a new style of architecture. Pitched roofs,

glass windows, and other accoutrements dressed up the impoverished-looking communities of the Southwest, at least in the eyes of the occupants. The railroad continued to speed up changes in the Southwest until people like Jesse Nusbaum, Sylvanus Morley, John Gaw Meem, along with a host of others, recognized the value of New Mexico's regional architecture. It was with their influence that the state saw the birth of the Pueblo Revival style in the early twentieth century.

Today, New Mexico is proud of her heritage, and many communities have passed regulations to protect the past from being erased by modern developments. New construction draws elements from the older buildings, with facades emulating earlier structures. The town of Santa Fe still has nar-

ABOVE: THE ADOBE MOSQUE AT ABIQUIÚ WAS DESIGNED BY EGYPTIAN ARCHITECT HASSAN FATHY. BUILT WITH ARCHES, VAULTS, AND DOMES BY EGYPTIAN MASONS AND VOLUNTEERS, THE BUILDING REFLECTS ARCHITECTURE FOUND IN THE ISLAMIC WORLD.

LEFT: ELABORATE WOOD CORBELS ARE PART OF THE ARCHITECTURAL DETAILING FOUND THROUGHOUT NEW MEXICO.

row streets in the city center that wind around in a haphazard manner. An architectural board reviews building plans to ensure compatibility with the rest of the town's structures. It is partly due to the effect of these rigid rules that New Mexico is now attracting a vast number of newcomers.

INSPIRATION FROM CHACO CANYON

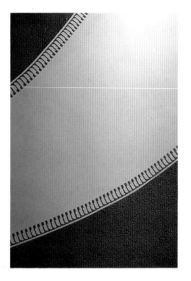

Bermed into a south-facing slope among piñon and juniper trees is the Santa Fe home of Joe and Valerie Bechtol. Patterned after Pueblo Bonito in Chaco Canyon in northwestern New Mexico, the house lies directly east of Bandelier National Monument, an area originally occupied by groups of Anasazi Indians.

The designer and builder, John McGowen, thought a great deal about ancient civilizations and how people lived with the forces of nature. Using both old and new technologies, McGowen strove to make the Bechtol house blend well with the environment and at the same time be aesthetically pleasing. The walls curve in snakelike fashion, with odd-shaped openings. The roof is made of sod, and a greenhouse space is attached to the southern section of the house. Large cottonwood trees provide protection and shade in the summer months and allow the sun to enter in the winter. The name of the house, Ahkon Povi, is a Tewa Indian name meaning "desert flower."

The adobe walls are two feet thick, except the back bermed wall. Vigas, naturally aged by a forest fire, span the ceilings, and twisted limbs of juniper are used as lintels above the window openings. Embedded in the wall are potsherds, which appear as a break between textures and colors on a wall surface. Everything in the house appears handcrafted.

TOP: WITH ITS SLOPING WALLS, THE HOUSE SEEMS TO BE PART OF THE NATURAL ENVIRONMENT. NATIVE PLANTS SURROUND THE HOUSE, AND LARGE DECIDUOUS TREES PROVIDE SUMMER SHADE FROM SOUTHERN EXPOSURE. FLAGSTONE WALKS EXTEND OUT FROM THE HOUSE AND AROUND THE EDGES OF THE GARDEN.

BOTTOM LEFT: SET INTO A SOUTH-FACING SLOPE, THE HOUSE USES THE EARTH FOR INSULATION AGAINST EXTREME TEMPERATURES.

BOTTOM RIGHT: A SHEPHERD'S FIREPLACE IN THE LIVING AREA IS AN ATTRACTIVE ELEMENT THAT OFFERS HEAT DURING THE COLD WINTER MONTHS.

A flagstone walk leads up to the greenhouse, a glass-enclosed space with a sitting area, a garden, and a Jacuzzi that is also a heat collector. In the winter, the sun beats through the clear roof panels onto the water and against the adobe wall, which acts as a storage battery, slowly absorbing heat and radiating it into the main living area of the house. The amount of heat transferred is regulated by fans. Low operable vents supply fresh air. The sitting area is used as a breakfast space in the summer and for lunches in the winter.

"One of the most interesting features of the house," explains Valerie Bechtol, "is the combination hot-water heater and space heater." The unit utilizes two moderate-sized solar collectors for the heat and a small photovoltaic cell to pump the water. A convection loop is an integral part of the apparatus. For heat control, the utilized air may be drawn from inside or outside the house, and the warm air blown inside or outside according to room temperature preference.

TOP: THE LIVING SPACE HAS BUILT-IN BANCOS, COVERED WITH CUSHIONS AND PILLOWS THAT FACE A LARGE SHEPHERD'S FIREPLACE. AN EXTENSIVE MASK COLLECTION HANGS ON THE WALLS. POTSHERDS COLLECTED NEARBY DECORATE THE ADOBE WALLS. SKYLIGHTS BATHE THE ROOM IN THE EVER-CHANGING LIGHT FROM THE SUN.

BOTTOM LEFT: A LOFT FUNCTIONS AS A PRIVATE CONVERSATION AREA OR SLEEPING SPACE. WINDOWS OPEN THE SMALL AREA TO THE VIEWS OF THE NEW MEXICAN LANDSCAPE AND SKIES.

BOTTOM RIGHT: SHELVES AND BANCOS ARE SCULPTURAL EXTENSIONS OF THE WALL, FORMED AND PLASTERED TO MATCH. LARGE VIGAS WERE NATURALLY AGED BY A FOREST FIRE, AND THE FLOORS ARE FLAGSTONE, A COMMON ELEMENT USED THROUGHOUT THE HOUSE.

Glass double doors open onto an internal communal space, called the great room, which includes a kitchen, an eating area, a living room, and a large shepherd's fireplace. Against two walls in the living area are white-plastered bancos, or benches, that are covered with cushions and pillows and used for seating around the fireplace. A slab of sandstone is built into the corner and functions as an end table. The kitchen is a sculptured space with free-form plastered shelves and a sink covered in odd pebble-shaped tiles. A small colorful table hugs the back wall and is used during spells of bad weather. Most of the ceilings in the great room have coved plaster between the vigas and recessed lighting that washes a pale yellow light across the walls. Skylights direct beams of sunlight into the room throughout the day.

A room-to-room floor plan eliminates the need for hallways. Adjacent to the great room is a den/bedroom, a simple space with a ladder that climbs up to a loft. Windows in the loft space have majestic views that capture the enormous skies of New Mexico.

The bathroom, which connects the den/ bedroom with the master bedroom, features a shower that has a floor lined with smooth black stones rounded by years of wear. Chipped pieces of turquoise tile cover the sink and countertop, and recessed shelving provides storage space.

In the master bedroom, free-flowing walls form three-dimensional sculpted shelves and night tables. A fireplace at the far end helps keep the room warm in winter.

Because they needed a studio space, the Bechtols decided to add a separate building at a higher level of the property that would also include guest quarters. The entryway doubles as a foyer for the guest house and a gallery off the studio space. The studio is a large utility space, easy to work in. The guest house is in keeping with the main house, with many handcrafted touches and south-facing windows to capture the winter sun.

Because of a rare understanding for the land and its history, John McGowen was able to create a living space that takes advantage of the site and meets all the Bechtols' needs.

A GREENHOUSE IS ATTACHED TO THE SOUTH SIDE OF THE BECHTOLS' HOUSE IN SANTA FE, TAKING ADVANTAGE OF THE DIRECT WINTER SUN. THE VIGAS ARE CRADLED BY METAL PLATES DECORATED WITH HAND-PAINTED INDIAN DESIGNS. FLAGSTONE STEPS LEAD TO A JACUZZI ON A HIGHER LEVEL OF THE GREENHOUSE.

HOUSE OF STRAW

LEFT: NEXT TO THE PROTECTIVE SLOPES OF A NARROW CANYON, THE CARABELLI HOME IN CHUPADERO, NORTH OF SANTA FE, IS CAREFULLY SITED TO TAKE ADVANTAGE OF ITS ENVIRONMENT. NATIVE CHAMISA SURROUNDS THE HOUSE MADE WITH STRAW. PORCHES ROOFED WITH CORRUGATED TIN WRAP AROUND TWO SIDES AND ARE HEATED BY AN OUTDOOR FIREPLACE.

RIGHT: WALLS MADE WITH BALES OF STRAW GO UP QUICKLY. DURING STACKING THEY ARE PINNED WITH REBAR, STEEL RODS USUALLY USED IN REINFORCED CONCRETE, OR WOODEN STAKES THAT HOLD THE COURSES TOGETHER.

In the late 1800s, people were homesteading the Sand Hills in central and western Nebraska. Trees were nonexistent, and even sod was at a premium. Shelter building required ingenuity. Families started using meadow hay — bundled, stacked, and pinned — for temporary housing. Eventually these houses were stuccoed inside and out, providing tremendous insulation from the long, hard winters. The straw worked so well that owners were reluctant to give it up and construct more conventional homes.

When Virginia Carabelli bought her property in Chupadero, north of Santa Fe, it was surrounded by Indian reservations on three sides. The site follows the course of a stream, down a narrow canyon fringed with cottonwoods. The house is protected from the flood-prone areas, built on higher ground against the slopes where piñon and juniper trees grow.

The house, based on the same principles as the late-nineteenth-century straw architecture of Nebraska, is the first residential structure made of bales of straw to receive a building permit in the United States. The state officials were intrigued by the idea, but insisted on certain conditions. The straw could only act as a filler for a post-and-beam structure, and tests had to prove that the straw did not present a fire hazard. Fortu-

nately, the densely packed bales only smoldered when tested.

There are numerous advantages to straw-bale houses. They are not expensive, mortar is unnecessary, and insulation in the thirty-inch walls has a rating between R-40 and R-50. The stuccoed straw has an irregular wall surface akin to old adobe but far less labor-intensive. Stacked and pinned with steel rods or wooden stakes, the bales can be made into walls in a day or two.

Straw also has ecological advantages. It is renewable waste that is usually baled, tilled under, or burned. Using straw bales could become an alternative to depleting old-growth forests or employing building products that are manufactured with fossil fuels, which contribute to the high carbon

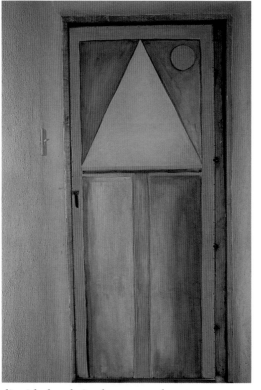

dioxide levels in the atmosphere.

The house is designed to adjust to the area's weather extremes. The main room is a simple rectangle paved with clay tiles that faces north and west, with deep porches on two sides that let in only low light. In the heat of the summer, five old Spanish Colonial double doors are kept open during the night to let the cooler air in. The porches are used as outdoor rooms. In the winter, an outdoor fireplace on the north porch helps keep it an active area. Shutters and doors control the amount of light, as well as the

amount of air — cold or hot — that enters the house.

Matts Myrhman, a straw-bale consultant in Tucson, advises potential straw-bale-home builders to study their climate carefully before deciding on the best technique for covering straw-bale walls. In humid environments, it is essential that the walls breathe; adobe plaster rather than concrete allows the moisture in the straw to evaporate. He also believes that straw can be a simple solution to many complex problems that may face home builders in the arid Southwest.

SANTA FE CONTEMPORARY

North of Santa Fe, on a high ridge with views of piñon, juniper, chamisa, and paintbrush, is the home of Melanie Peters. Ingenuity and creative thinking were required to take full advantage of the climate and landscape. "Since the land slopes north with views to the east and west, it is a difficult site sunwise," explains architect Bob Zachry. A collaborative effort between the client and the architect resulted in a T-shaped design that lines up in all four directions. The public space is on a north-south axis and opens to the east and west. Deep portales screen the house from the heat and direct sunlight. For winter warmth, the sleeping area is in the secluded south-facing wing.

"In the public space," explains Bob Zachry, "we used doors instead of windows. Indoor-outdoor circulation was a priority." Seven pairs of wood-framed glass doors line up on both *portales*. Weathered antique Mexican doors were used for the front entry.

The living room, kitchen and breakfast area, and dining room occupy one large space, with different floor levels giving each section a different feeling. The living room on the north end of the house stretches out from east to west with twelve-foot-high beamed ceilings stained a light brown. A fireplace with a fresh-air vent is the central focal point; it is set off by smooth-troweled

plaster. The walls are the natural color of the plaster, which is a light fleshy tone, warm and reflective. "Inside, I wanted a monochromatic color scheme with light stains highlighted by more colorful furnishings, artwork, pillows, and rugs," explains the owner.

Several stairs lead up to the higher level of the kitchen and breakfast area and dining room, with a low half-curving wall providing a break between the breakfast area and the living room. The kitchen and breakfast areas are linked together as one continuous space. Two pairs of glass doors lead from the dining area to the west portal, where tables, chairs, and a Taos bed allow for comfort-

able outdoor living. All the glass doors to both portals can be opened, expanding the internal space to the outside gardens.

In the center of the T is the library — a comfortable space that can double as a guest bedroom. A south-facing window opens up to the landscape and keeps the room warm in the cooler months.

The guest room contains the only interior surfaces that use strong colors — a deep sage green and peach. Large windows and a single glass door face the south portal with a view of potted flowers, coyote fencing, and the skies beyond. The master suite uses lighter, more subtle shades. It has a corner

THE LIVING ROOM HAS HIGH BEAMED CEILINGS AND CEMENT-TILE FLOORS. LIGHT POURS IN FROM SEVERAL PAIRS OF GLASS DOORS THAT LEAD TO EAST AND WEST PORCHES. ECLECTIC FURNISHINGS, INCLUDING AN AFRICAN END TABLE COVERED IN ZEBRA HIDE, CENTER ON THE FIREPLACE. BETWEEN TWO SOFAS COVERED IN LEE JOFA CHENILLE IS A MARBLE-BASE COFFEE TABLE ON TOP OF A MOROCCAN TRIBAL RUG. TALL, GRACEFUL YUCCAS FLANK EACH SIDE OF THE ROOM.

fireplace and a pair of glass doors that open to the east portal and patio.

In contrast to the interior, the outside of the house has a more dramatic color scheme. Influenced by Luis Barragán and tempered by the Santa Fe style, Melanie Peters used earth tones that play off one another, changing as the light changes. The chimney be-comes a vertical stripe of burnt sienna. The portals have walls a shade of salmon and a cream color ceiling with the doors stained to match. Teal-blue trim contrasts with the desert-rose wall that faces the street. Around the perimeter of the yard are low walls that delineate the more formal gardens on the east and west sides.

"The low walls are a way of defining the watered area, which is like a little oasis, without interrupting the views," says Bob Zachry. Beyond the walls, wild areas with wildflowers and piñon and juniper trees stretch out in all directions to the distant mountains.

EARTHSHIPS

LEFT: COWBOY FURNISHINGS
AND NAVAJO RUGS DECORATE
THE WEAVERS' HOUSE, LOCATED
NEAR TAOS. A FIREPLACE WITH A
FRESH-AIR VENT HEATS THE
HOUSE.

RIGHT: THE SHAPE OF THE
TIRES, USED IN THE CONSTRUC-
TION OF THE WEAVER HOME,
FORMS A SOFT-EDGED WALL THAT
FLOWS EASILY INTO A BUILT-IN
BANCO IN THE LIVING ROOM.

In Taos, Michael Reynolds is design-ing what he calls Earthships, self-sufficient structures built from mostly recycled materials, such as old tires and alu-minum cans. These are packed and plastered with earth and have south-facing solar walls.

Reynolds has conceptualized a method of construction that will eventually sever the need to rely on outside sources of power, sewage disposal, or water, eliminating the drain on our natural resources. Rammed earth in steel-belted tires and aluminum cans, with the addition of bermed earth, form three sides of the U-shaped modules, while the fourth side is a south-facing glass wall that collects energy from the sun and is augmented by photovoltaic panels. Adobe plaster is used to finish the surface of the walls, creating a smooth plaster coat that resembles that of a conventional adobe home.

Twenty years ago Michael Reynolds saw a link between the rising cost of housing and the overwhelming problem of waste. He be-gan experimenting with aluminum cans and later added tires and rammed earth to cre-ate wall masses that have the capacity to hold heat like a storage battery, particularly when the house is partially submerged in a south-facing slope. When incorporating a green-house space along the south glass wall, an Earthship can provide a year-round food

TOP: THE UNFINISHED EXTERIOR OF AN EARTHSHIP REVEALS THE ALUMINUM CANS AND TIRES THAT WERE RECYCLED TO CONSTRUCT ITS WALLS. (PHOTO BY SUZI MOORE)

MIDDLE: MADE OF BOTTLES AND ADOBE PLASTER, THE WEAVERS' BATHROOM EMITS A MUTED INTERIOR LIGHT.

BOTTOM: ALUMINUM CANS COVERED WITH PLASTER BECOME FILLER AND INTERIOR WALLS.

supply. The greenhouse space also functions as a corridor for the U-shaped structure and as a heat distributor when the tire walls release their passively stored energy. For ventilation, low operable window vents in the glass wall breathe in the fresh air, while operable skylights in the highest rear point of the structures draw the warmer air up and out, like a chimney.

Cisterns collect snowmelt and rainwater and then filter them for household use. A graywater system, or a filtered holding tank, recycles all the water, except the toilet water, for use in the greenhouse. Reynolds is currently working on a waterless solar toilet, which will produce ash as an end product that can be used for fertilizer.

"From an environmental standpoint it's

an ideal method of construction," says actor Dennis Weaver, owner of two Earthships. "We took a problem and turned it into an asset. There are approximately two hundred and forty million tires discarded every year.

PRECEDING PAGES: BUILT FROM TIRES AND ALUMINUM CANS, THE HOUSE OF PAT HABITCH GLOWS WITH LIGHT AS EVENING APPROACHES.

That's one tire per person. We have a lot of waste products out there, and tires are indestructible. You ram it full of dirt until it weighs four hundred pounds, giving you a huge brick encased in steel, rubber, and syn-thetics. We use these bricks like ordinary bricks to build spaces. They make a strong house that requires no air-conditioning or heating, and we have a clean inexhaustible source of energy."

Dennis and Gerry Weaver have just finished a house on the slopes of the Sangre de Cristo Mountains above Taos that has endless views across the valley to the distant mountain ranges. The tires make a soft-cornered wall that rolls out of the surrounding earth and into a glass wall. The glass is perpendicular to the rays of the lowest winter sun, which hits the massive storage walls in the winter, but not in the summer. Earthship plans are adaptable to hot or cold climates by subtle variations that include changing the angle of the glass.

Inside the Weaver house, glass bottle bottoms are used for a planter wall in the greenhouse and as a bathroom wall on the upper level. Aluminum cans plastered with adobe create partial interior walls or stairwells and are used for filler. During construction nothing was thrown out. It was a constant process of recycling. The Weavers have sixteen solar panels to run their house, panels that actually powered the tools used during construction, reducing the need for an electric company.

"We have no motors or fans going," explains Dennis Weaver. "It's such a natural feeling. We live with our house, which becomes a joy — functioning with our environment instead of defiling it." Even the refrigerator is run by solar panels.

The Weavers support and participate in a cleaner way of living in today's world by using alternative solutions that are harmonious with their southwestern landscape. They are part of a growing minority that is not afraid to cast aside conventional ideas in favor of more experimental approaches to the ever-increasing environmental problems facing our world.

THE NATURAL WOOD IN THE WEAVERS' HANDCRAFTED KITCHEN CONTRASTS WITH THE DARKER ADOBE PLASTER. A SOLAR-POWERED REFRIGERATOR AND LIGHTS MAKE THE NEED FOR AN ELECTRIC COMPANY OBSOLETE.

THE STAIRWAY IN THE WEAVERS'
HOUSE LEADS TO AN UPPER
LEVEL WITH TWO BEDROOMS
AND A BATHROOM. WALLS ACT
AS STORAGE BATTERIES,
COLLECTING THE HEAT FROM
THE SUN THAT POURS THROUGH
THE SOUTH-FACING WINDOWS.
FLOORS THROUGHOUT
THE HOUSE ARE MADE OF
FLAGSTONE.

TEXAS

Stretching out across varied landscapes, west Texas changes dramatically from east to west and north to south. Unlike other states in the Southwest region, west Texas often experiences significant climate fluctuations in a short period of time. The weather is unpredictable. Temperatures have been known to plummet fifty degrees in a thirty-six-hour period. It is a place of droughts and floods, tornados and cold northern winds.

In the far southwestern part of the state is the Basin and Range region, also known as the Trans-Pecos, characterized by the southern end of the Rocky Mountains, flat desert basins flooded by the light of an unyielding sun, and spectacular canyons, including those in Big Bend National Park. During spring and after summer rains, the land explodes with seasonal wildflowers: prickly poppies, desert lantana, penstemon, and paintbrush.

To the south is the lower Rio Grande valley, known for its citrus and other crops. The Rio Grande — the border between Texas and Mexico — irrigates the lowland. Inland, remote ranches lie nestled in the middle of mesquite thickets and grassland. Deer and armadillos hide in the thorny brush while caracaras hover overhead.

The central and western High Plains are made up of rolling hills and deep valleys, treeless prairies and lush grasslands, limestone bedrock and stunted shrubbery, and strong

winds and swirling dust. It was this land and the rest of western Texas that attracted explorers early in American history.

During the eighteenth century, while France was creeping across the eastern edges of Texas, Spain was busy establishing a chain of missions to increase her hold on the entire region. But even then, Spain was not satisfied and decided to send Don Martin de Alarcón with fifty soldiers to establish a

ABOVE: THE RIO GRANDE WINDS ITS WAY THROUGH SANTA ELENA CANYON AT BIG BEND NATIONAL PARK IN SOUTHWESTERN TEXAS.

LEFT: A MOORISH ARCH FRAMES THE ENTRANCE TO THE MISSION SAN FRANCISCO DE LA ESPADA ON THE SOUTHERN EDGE OF SAN ANTONIO. A THREE-BELL TOWER CROWNS THE STONE FACADE OF THE CHURCH. BUILT IN 1756 BY SPAIN, IT IS PART OF THE MISSION TRAIL ESTABLISHED IN TEXAS DURING THE EIGHTEENTH CENTURY.

PRECEDING PAGES: WINDMILLS AND ROLLING GRASSLANDS ARE PART OF THE LANDSCAPE SURROUNDING BURNET, NORTHWEST OF AUSTIN, TEXAS.

presidio and mission between the San Antonio and San Pedro Rivers as a halfway point to eastern Texas. This mission, Mission San Antonio de Valero, is better known today as the Alamo. The original presidio was constructed with thatched

buildings, which were later replaced by more permanent adobe structures. This was the beginning of the mission trail that came to include Mission Concepción, Mission San José, Mission San Juan de los Nazonis, and Mission San Francisco de la Espada. Mission architecture in Texas reflected Spanish architectural history, with visible Moorish, Gothic, and Renaissance details, altered by the availability of materials.

By 1821, Mexico had achieved independence from Spain, allowing settlement in Texas by Anglos who were willing or said they were willing to become Mexican citizens and embrace the Catholic religion. The advantage of going to Texas rather than other areas of the United States was the reasonable price of land, which was Mexico's method of encouraging colonization. Alsatians, Germans, and Scandinavians came to the area; skilled at stonemasonry, these settlers built permanent houses with pitched roofs, using local limestone and timber. In fourteen years the population in Texas increased from a handful to thirty-five thousand, thirty thousand of whom were Anglos, who soon tired of being ruled by Mexico.

The 1835 battle for Texas independence resulted in Texas's being an independent republic for more than ten years before annexation to the United States in 1845 and the Mexican War in 1846. For years, cotton and cattle were the principal products of Texas and the state's economic base. Then as Texans accumulated wealth and the railroad developed, Texas architecture began to change. Fancy scrolls and lacework were added to stately homes to give a Victorian touch, and sprawling ranch houses were built on the vast prairies. The oil boom brought more money into the state, and not long after the turn of the century, farms, ranches, urban expansion, and oil changed the face of the Texas frontier forever.

Today, modern west Texas architecture has adopted a regional approach to design: thick limestone walls keep the interiors cool in summer and warm in winter, homes are constructed with the angles of the sun in mind, and windows and doors are aligned to take full advantage of breezes for cross-ventilation. These houses are structures built to incorporate the natural elements, while working within the strict confines of their environment.

ABOVE: PET LONGHORNS REST UNDER THE SHADE OF MESQUITE TREES OUTSIDE BURNET.

LEFT: AIRY MOUNT, NAMED FOR ITS WINDY LOCATION ON THE HIGHEST POINT OF LAND IN THE IMMEDIATE AREA, WAS BUILT IN 1884 BY CONFEDERATE GENERAL A. R. JOHNSON. TWENTY-FOUR-INCH-THICK LIMESTONE WALLS HELP KEEP THE HOUSE COOL. OVER EACH LONG AND NARROW DOUBLE-HUNG WINDOW IS A STONE LINTEL WITH A KEYSTONE. AS EVIDENCED BY CERTAIN ARCHITECTURAL ELEMENTS, SUCH AS FINIALS, TRUSSES, AND LACY BRACKETS AND RAILINGS, THE HOUSE IS A MIXTURE OF GOTHIC REVIVAL AND VICTORIAN STYLES.

HISTORIC LIMESTONE

LEFT: VINTAGE FURNISHINGS COMPLEMENT THIS HISTORIC LIMESTONE HOUSE. TWO RUSTIC SOFAS COVERED IN LEATHER FACE EACH OTHER IN FRONT OF THE FIREPLACE IN THE LIVING ROOM. A CEILING FAN CIRCULATES THE AIR, AND SHUTTERED WINDOWS CONTROL THE AMOUNT OF SUNLIGHT AND AIR THAT ENTERS THE ROOM. A VINTAGE COLLECTION OF COWBOY BOOTS DECORATES THE MANTEL OF THE FIREPLACE. PROFESSIONAL COLLECTORS, THE BEARDS OWN A COMPANY CALLED TRUE WEST THAT SUPPLIES COWBOYANA TO PEOPLE ALL OVER THE COUNTRY, INCLUDING RALPH LAUREN'S POLO STORES.

RIGHT: VINTAGE NAVAJO BLANKETS AND RUGS DECORATE THE HOUSE.

In 1984, Tyler and Teresa Beard discovered their Texas dream house in the town of Comanche. Recognizing the architectural value of an 1886 limestone house that had been vacant for more than forty years, they purchased it despite its dilapidated condition. There were no bathrooms, no septic system, and no electricity. The stove and stovepipe had been removed from the kitchen, leaving a gaping hole in the roof where the rain had poured through, rotting the floorboards and washing out sections of the kitchen walls.

The restoration took a year. Four hundred trees were removed from the property before the house could even be seen from the street. The limestone walls were left exposed both inside and out. Every window was taken out, patched and painted, fitted with new glass, and put back in again. After forty years not much paint remained on anything; luckily, all the wood trim in the house is cypress, which is not prone to rot. Old bricks were purchased through the Fort Worth stockyards to replace the rotted kitchen floor. A bathroom was built in an existing kitchen storeroom.

Today, large pecan trees shade the front of the house, and vines cling to the great limestone walls, protecting them from the heat of the day. Limestone walks were laid on top of old dirt paths. A picket fence en-

closes the side yard and outlines the boundaries on that side of the land.

The original owners understood the need to design a house for this climate. The front entry opens onto a zaguan that connects the front yard to the rear patio with interior doors off each side. Transoms are used above the outside doors for cross-ventilation. "Everything lines up so the breezes can blow through, which is aided by old Indian-style shutters that control the heat and light. We have five exit doors and fifteen windows," says Tyler Beard. The doors and windows face each other throughout the house.

The south-facing master bedroom has a wood-front fireplace that keeps the room warm during the three winter months. Two windows on each side of the fireplace face south, letting in the winter sun, and two windows face west, warming the room before the evening. Another window faces east and lets in the early morning sun.

TOP: TYLER BEARD LAID A LIMESTONE WALK ON THE BACK PATIO. VINES, LARGE TREES, AND A PORCH SHADE THE WALLS OF THE HOUSE FROM THE INTENSE SUMMER SUN. THE ORIGINAL TIN ROOF PROVIDES A REFLECTIVE SURFACE THAT KEEPS RAIN OFF THE LIMESTONE WALLS.

BOTTOM: A HIGH PATIO FENCE AND LANDSCAPING CREATE PRIVATE OUTDOOR LIVING SPACES. THE LANDSCAPED WALK LEADS TO THE BACK ENTRANCE.

TOP: A ROLL-DOWN CANVAS SHADE ON THE SOUTH END OF THE BACK PORCH SCREENS OUT UNWANTED SUNLIGHT AND BREEZES. THE PORCH IS AN EXTENDED AREA OF THE HOUSE FOR LIVING AND DINING.

BOTTOM: THE BEARDS COMMISSIONED RONNIE MARTIN IN GRAHAM, TEXAS, TO MAKE OUTDOOR HORSESHOE FURNITURE FOR AN AREA OF THE BACK PATIO UNDER A SPREADING SHADE TREE.

The living room is a reverse of the bedroom, with a fireplace on the north wall and windows flanking each side. A door to the dining room lines up with one of the two west windows, both of which are shaded by a large pecan tree in the summer.

There are no hallways. It's a room-to-room layout that forms an L, with one space moving into the next, indicative of nineteenth-century architecture. The dining room attaches to the kitchen, which is in the easternmost portion of the house. The sun bathes the room with a warm morning glow that filters through a narrow double-hung window, but before the heat has a chance to take hold, the sun moves around to the other side of the house. Tyler Beard notes, "It was planned so the sun would not reach the kitchen during the heat of the day, since that's when the cooking would be done."

On the rear patio is a porch thirty feet long and ten feet wide. A limestone walk

leads from the porch to the back of the fenced yard, where under the shade of an enormous pecan tree is a sitting area with horseshoe furniture made by Ronnie Martin of Graham, Texas.

The Beards want their home to be a reflection of the area in which they live. Vintage coffee tins sit on top of an antique jam cabinet in the kitchen, fringed leather pillows decorate sofas and chairs in the living room, nostalgic western blankets are casually draped over the end of the bed. Throughout the house, the furnishings are characteristic of the region.

ABOVE: AN OLD JAM CUPBOARD AND A COLLECTION OF VINTAGE TINS MAKE THE EATING AREA IN THE KITCHEN COLORFUL. HANGING ON THE WALL BEHIND THE SINK IS AN OLD NAVAJO BLANKET. COWBOYANA, ANTIQUES, AND BLANKETS BLEND WELL WITH THE HISTORIC LIMESTONE RESTORATION. SHUTTERED WINDOWS HELP CONTROL THE HEAT AND LIGHT.

RIGHT: OLD NAVAJO BLANKETS, PERIOD PIECES, AND ANTIQUE FURNITURE FILL THE DINING ROOM. CUSTOM-MADE GALVANIZED LIGHTING FIXTURES HANG FROM THE CEILING. BRANDING IRONS ARE USED FOR CANDLESTICKS IN THE CENTER OF THE DINING ROOM TABLE.

TEXAS GARDEN HOUSE

James David and Gary Peese's unusual house in Austin acknowledges the area's architectural roots through the use of limestone. It also demonstrates the successful integration of house and landscape. "The house is the nucleus, and the garden an extension that grows out from the core," explains Austin-based landscape architect James David. The house, which sits on the highest point of its site, was planned by architect James Coote and built in the early 1980s. A new limestone addition was designed by architect Paul Lamb.

The landscape dramatically falls away in all directions. Terraces linked by limestone steps, landings, and garden paths support the architecture as entertainment areas that expand the living space beyond the walls.

The garden has the same features as the architecture, with a progression of spaces formally set up with horizontal and vertical planes that have repetitive lines and forms. The unfenced back area has a different landscape from the other gardens, one that does not tempt the pillaging of armadillos and deer, a major problem in the area.

When Coote designed the original house, he told the owners that he was influenced by farmhouses in Europe. Rather than design a reproduction, however, he would use the "essence without the mimicry." The spaces are large and have a sense of sophis-

tication without being fancy.

In the front, cracked limestone blocks cover the floor of the porch and continue through the main entry, establishing a continuity in materials that builds a relationship among the different functions of the spaces. The foyer opens onto a two-story living room; attached is a dining area. A pair of doors opens or closes off the library on the north side, adjacent to a stairway that climbs up to the bedroom wing. There are no architectural boundaries; each space relates to the next.

Three years ago David, who is also the owner of a garden and design shop, and Peese, a gourmet cook, completed a two-story addition with a new kitchen and small bedroom. Architect Paul Lamb did not try to match the original structure, but instead chose to integrate the new with the old by using complementary materials — limestone in contrast to smooth plaster, sheet-metal roofing against clay tiles, and wood floors next to stone.

Double French doors connect the new kitchen with the original house. The floors are longleaf yellow pine, and the ceilings use tongue-and-groove pine boards painted a soft sage. Along the west wall a low bank of square windows keeps the focal point down in the valley rather than higher up, where power lines intersect the view. The windows also provide interior light without late-afternoon glare. Buttermilk-colored paint

TOP LEFT: AN OUTDOOR DINING AREA WITH VIEWS OF THE BACK GARDEN IS ATTACHED TO THE KITCHEN. A COUNT RUMFORD FIREPLACE — A SHALLOW FIREPLACE DESIGNED TO THROW HEAT INTO A ROOM — GIVES OFF ENOUGH HEAT TO MAKE THIS A COMFORTABLE PLACE IN COOLER WEATHER. LIMESTONE BLOCKS PAVE THE PORCH AND CONTINUE DOWN INTO THE GARDEN.

TOP RIGHT: A SMALL GARDEN TOWER RISING FROM THE BACK PATIO IS REMINISCENT OF SPANISH ARCHITECTURE DURING THE OCCUPATION OF THE MOORS. LIMESTONE TERRACES, LANDINGS, AND STEPS LEAD TO UNFENCED AREAS.

BOTTOM: THE BEDROOM ADDITION BENEATH THE NEW KITCHEN PROVIDES A SANCTUARY FROM THE REST OF THE HOUSE. A BUILT-IN BED IS SET INTO A DRAPED SLEEPING ALCOVE THAT HAS SHELVING FOR BOOKS.

covers the cabinets and walls, a reflective surface that changes color in the afternoon sun.

Attached to the kitchen is a covered dining porch and outdoor fireplace that overlook the back garden and surrounding countryside. Limestone blocks pave the floor and also the stairs that lead down to the new

bedroom and bathroom and the lower levels of the garden. The bedroom is an intimate space using yellows and grays. There is only an outside entrance, a single French door that connects with the west garden and guarantees privacy from the rest of the house. The floor is cut limestone, aged under oak trees and stained with tannic acid and tree pollen — a textured surface that absorbs moisture from the shower. Two asymmetrical windows provide light and views across the back patio.

Outside, a detached grape arbor is supported by concrete posts and a steel-pipe framework across the top. Black Spanish grapes and *Thunbergia grandiflora* climb up and over, shading the sitting area below.

Hills crowded with oak and thick brush, amid which sit carefully sited houses, surround the perimeter of the property. "I want the architecture to be connected to the region I live in," says David. "I want it to look like it belongs in Austin and grows out of the community. I'm constantly reevaluating and editing what I see, constantly simplifying. That's my art, the art of landscaping."

EASY TO USE, THE GOURMET KITCHEN HAS A CENTER ISLAND AND OPEN STORAGE SPACE. NATURAL LONGLEAF-YELLOW-PINE FLOORS AND A TONGUE-AND-GROOVE CEILING PAINTED SAGE ARE COMPLEMENTED BY THE BUTTERMILK-YELLOW CABINETS.

CONTEMPORARY RANCH HOUSE

The architectural team of David Lake and Ted Flato in San Antonio has a unique understanding of the kind of vernacular architecture appropriate to the southern Texas climate and landscape. As evidenced by the Lasater home near Hebbronville, their designs incorporate historical traditions with regional materials woven together by skilled craftsmen.

The house is an L-shaped compound joined by a common roof and a screened porch that faces into the breezes blowing off the adjacent pond. "Garland Lasater liked to camp at his ranch in a tent and wanted the design of the house to have a similar relationship with the outdoors," explains project director Flato. "He wanted a way to live outside year-round."

Rolling barn doors slide across two ends of the screened porch, protecting the outside room from the cold northern winds in the wintertime. At the same time, the winter sun fills the porch with warmth and light. A cozy fireplace in a barbecue area provides outside heat. If the weather is unusually cold, the Lasaters can retreat into the interior core, a space insulated by thick storage walls, which contains a kitchen and small sitting and eating areas. Pairs of glass doors span eight-by-eight-foot openings on three sides. A high center cupola has operable vents that inhale fresh air, while ceiling fans keep the air circulating in the rooms.

At each end of the L shape are sleeping spaces that can be shut off from the rest of the house and artificially cooled on hot summer nights. When the weather is mild the screened area can also be used as a sleeping porch.

Materials are simple. The corrugated metal roof is shaped much like that of a Texas barn, steeper in the middle and flattened out toward the ends. The porch floors are brick on sand for easy maintenance, while Saltillo tiles are used in the interior core. The ceilings are tongue-and-groove pine boards.

"Stucco is used inside and out to make a connection between the two spaces," says Flato. "And when the doors of the center core are opened up, it becomes part of the porch, which is like a *palapa*, or open porch, in Mexico, except you need the screening in Texas."

The transition to the outside flows eas-

TOP: SLEEPING SPACES ON EITHER END OF THE COMPOUND CAN BE SHUT OFF FROM THE REST OF THE HOUSE AND ARTIFICIALLY COOLED ON HOT NIGHTS. TONGUE-AND-GROOVE PLANKS COVER THE WALLS AND CEILING. SIMPLE FURNISHINGS DECORATE THE ROOM.

BOTTOM: WITH ITS SCREENED LIVING SPACES, THE HOUSE OPENS WIDE TO THE VIBRANT NIGHT SKIES OF TEXAS.

TOP: THE MAIN INTERIOR SECTION OF THE HOUSE CONTAINS AN OPEN KITCHEN, A SMALL SITTING SPACE, AND AN EATING AREA. INSULATED STORAGE WALLS KEEP THE CORE WARM IN THE WINTER. WHEN THE DOORS ARE OPEN TO THE BREEZEWAY AND THE SCREENED LIVING PORCH, THE CIRCULATING AIR KEEPS THIS SPACE COOL IN THE SUMMER.

BOTTOM: MAKING UP THE CONVERSATION AREA ON THE PORCH IS *EQUIPALE*, OR MEXICAN PIGSKIN FURNITURE, WITH CUSHIONS MADE OUT OF NATURAL FABRICS. ON COOL EVENINGS, THE FIREPLACE PROVIDES HEAT, AND ROLLING BARN DOORS CLOSE OFF THIS SIDE OF THE HOUSE FROM THE NORTHERN WINDS.

ily, with open breezeways and screened living spaces that carry the architecture beyond the house. Outside, acacia and mesquite trees grow in thickets not far from the house, and black-eyed Susans line the banks of the pond. Close to the house are yuccas, *cenizo*, or Texas sage, and other regional plants.

Both the Lasaters come from old Texas families, were born in San Antonio, and have deep roots connecting them to the area.

"My connection with the land has become more important since we've lived here," says Mollie Lasater. "We live on our porch. It's where we spend all our time, and where I like to sit and read. My favorite eating place is on the round table in front of the fireplace. It's designed as a gathering spot where we often have eight to ten people for dinner. That's how we like to use the house, with a lot of family and friends."

LA ESTRELLA

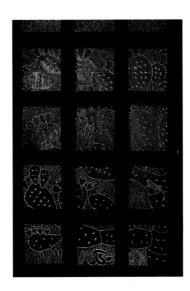

Tommy Funk worked with architect David Lake of Lake and Flato to create La Estrella, a compound whose materials and style emulate those of 1880s border architecture found in nearby Roma and Rio Grande City. Funk and Lake chose details from and techniques used for local buildings. The project included the remodeling of two existing structures from the 1970s and the addition of two new spaces. Together they form a hacienda-style compound with deep wraparound porches connecting the buildings around a central courtyard.

The existing mesquites as well as other native trees were left in place to create shade.

The north side of the compound deflects cold northern winds up and over the buildings, while the southeast side receives summer breezes. Shading the house like a giant sombrero, the porch is a comfortable extension of the interior living space.

Materials were found locally or at nearby sources. The walls of the new buildings are made with irregular Mexican bricks from a factory thirty miles away. The bricks are low fire and absorptive with wild variations in their natural color; for La Estrella they were covered with a paint made from pigments found in Mexico mixed with buttermilk and lime. "After application," explains David Lake, "the porous bricks sucked up a lot of pigment, leaving a uniformly bleached paint job resembling an old stucco wall in Mexico." For the floor in the master bedroom, a nearby steam-powered sawmill cut the mesquite planks, which came from timber on the Funk ranch and had been aged a year before use. Outside the compound old mesquite fence posts were used to create new fencing, another element common along this part of the Texas-Mexico border. Fireplaces were copied from some of the ruins in Roma and Rio Grande City. The roof is corrugated metal.

Galvanized-metal lighting fixtures and front-door panels were designed by Graham Martin and David Lake around the theme of local flora and fauna. Outside the compound, there are usually woodpeckers, cac-tus wrens, and caracaras gliding, diving, or riding the thermals. Orioles nest in the handcrafted lights hanging from the porch.

The remodeled main house includes a kitchen, living room, dining room, and spare bedroom with bathroom. A front porch protects this part of the compound from the intense summer sun, while providing a pleasant space to sit in the morning or evening.

The new family room, actually a separate

TOP: LARGE MESQUITES AND OTHER NATIVE TREES WERE LEFT IN THE COURTYARD FOR SHADE.

BOTTOM: OLD MESQUITE FENCE POSTS ENCLOSE THE AREA AROUND THE COMPOUND. WALLS OF THE NEW BUILDINGS ARE MADE FROM IRREGULAR MEXICAN BRICKS THAT COME FROM A NEARBY BORDER TOWN. THE PIGMENTS FOR THE WALLS WERE FOUND IN MEXICO AND MIXED WITH BUTTERMILK AND LIME, A PAINT THAT WAS READILY ABSORBED BY THE BRICKS, GIVING THE ILLUSION OF VERY OLD WALLS THAT HAD BLEACHED WITH AGE.

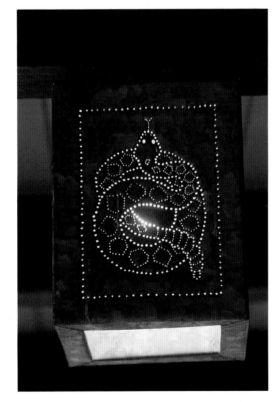

building, is patterned after a Mexican *bodega*, or granary, which was prevalent around the border areas in the 1880s. It has two ends with triangular parapets that were histori-cally designed to function as fire-stops. High granary windows are on the wall facing the outside, while the opposite wall has two pairs of double doors opening to the courtyard.

A new bedroom was added to the other section of the compound along with a mirador, or lookout, on the roof, surrounded by low walls. The lookout is patterned after the Rio Grande police station. The ceiling of the new bedroom is a *bóveda*, or fired-brick ceiling, common to northern Mexico. It is not a true vault or dome, but is laid free-form without the aid of supports. All the bedrooms have their own bathrooms and open onto the courtyard. An enclosed stair-way leads up to the roof, where a great view-ing area with built-in bancos overlooks the surrounding countryside.

The master suite, with details taken from the historic La Borde House in Rio Grande City, sits unattached to the rest of the structure on the east side of the compound. It is a large room with a small enclosed patio on one end and tall windows that look across the ranch on the other. On the courtyard side a door leads to an open porch with a half wall and a view of the rest of the ranch.

Even on close inspection the buildings truly look as if they have been there a hundred years, which is exactly what Funk had envisioned. The house combines local architectural features with indigenous materials, providing a contemporary living environment with historical roots. Climate also influenced the design, which is sheltered to the north and opens to the southeast, a realistic approach to building in a hot, dry area.

A RESTORED DINING ROOM IN THE ORIGINAL MAIN HOUSE INCORPORATES IDEAS AND STYLE USED IN THE NEW ADDITION.

ARIZONA

Arizona, home of the Grand Canyon, has four different deserts crossing its borders, resulting in vibrant landscapes teeming with distinctive biotic communities. The Mohave Desert, which moves in from southeastern California, is an intermediate zone somewhere between the Sonoran and the Great Basin Deserts, with characteristics of both.

Only a finger of the Chihuahuan Desert comes across from New Mexico, dominated by creosote bushes, needle-sharp yuccas, scrub mesquites, sandpaper bushes, and more than a thousand endemic plant species. It is a high desert, with layers of limestone covering 80 percent of its land.

The Great Basin Desert, also a high desert, encompasses the colorful sandstone buttes, mesas, and spires of northeastern Arizona and a small area in northwestern Arizona. Canyons dissect the plateau region and are expanded in size by rivers that continually eat away at the soil. There is spotty coverage of sagebrush, rabbitbrush, saltbush, prickly pear cacti.

The Sonoran Desert receives the greatest amount of rainfall and is the most diversified of the four deserts. High temperatures prevail. Two of its six subdivisions intrude into Arizona: the Arizona Upland and the lower Colorado River valley. Large trees and cacti mixed with low scrub and wild-

flowers grow on lowlands, uplands, and bajadas.

In June, the summer heat produces a penetratingly hot light that can be unrelenting. There is little hope of rain, not until July or maybe August. That is when temperatures keep build-

ing, as do the clouds — thick, dark cumulus clouds. Electric charges light up the sky, and the roar of thunder echoes throughout the region. Winds pick up, stirring the dust into tall masses that spin faster and faster, and finally one large water drop and then another falls, until the sky seems to open up,

ABOVE: YAQUI INDIANS HELPED SUPPLY THE LABOR FOR THIS HANDCRAFTED HOUSE BY WILL SCHUSTER IN TUCSON. BUILT FOR THE WRITER MURIEL PAINTER, THE DESIGN INCORPORATES ELEMENTS FROM THE EL SANCTUARIO CHURCH IN CHIMAYO, NEW MEXICO, INCLUDING BEAM CEILINGS WITH CARVED CORBELS.

BELOW: IN BARRIO VIEJO, AN OLD SONORAN-STYLE ROW HOUSE HAS INSULATING ADOBE WALLS. LOW-WATER-USE PLANTS, SUCH AS THE PRICKLY PEAR AND MEXICAN BIRD-OF-PARADISE, ARE PLANTED AGAINST THE OUTSIDE WALLS.

leaving enough water for a year in a matter of minutes. Arroyos fill dangerously full, and sheets of water wash away precious soils on flat ground. This desert is marked by a climatic madness. From time to time it even snows; too much snow or a dip too low in temperature can kill the giant saguaro, as can excessive rain. Snows are more common in the Great Basin Desert, which is both a warm and cold desert with plants especially adapted for either climate.

People have also adapted. The Hohokam, or ancient Canal Builders, devised systems to irrigate the desert so they could grow corn, beans, and squash. They also constructed shelters to shield them from the sun, pit houses that eventually grew into multistoried adobe apartment complexes. They were an enterprising people who had disappeared by A.D. 1450.

Lured by the promise of gold, the Spaniards appeared in present-day Arizona in the early 1500s with soldiers and missionaries eager to convert the native populations. The missionaries were unsuccessful with the Hopi in the north, but had better relations with the Pima, Tohono O'odham, Maricopa, and Yuma tribes in the southern half of the state. It

was not until 1692, beginning with Father Eusebio Kino, a Jesuit priest, that successful mission work helped colonize new areas. He brought in seeds and grains, new methods of farming, cattle and sheep ranching, and more precise tools that helped refine the architecture.

During this time the Apache were becoming more and more aggressive toward the settlers. A presidio was established by the Spaniards at Tubac, but as problems increased in other areas the site was moved to Tucson. Using techniques developed at mission sites, adobe walls measuring more than three feet at the base and twelve feet in height were built around the presidio. The living quarters were also built with adobe, an abundant material that was well suited for the desert climate. Thick walls with few openings, designed to work on the principal of thermal mass, insulated the interiors from the heat and cold. Ceilings used saguaro ribs and earth, two materials readily available. The roofs were flat and shed dust and debris that filtered onto the dirt floors. These were the early Sonoran-style houses; later they featured pitched roofs, wood floors, and porches.

DESERT RETREAT

Between two hills in a remote area of southern Arizona is the handcrafted sanctuary of writer Byrd Baylor. Its wavering adobe walls, rough-sawed lumber, and simple spaces resemble those of houses in rural Mexico. The house represents the collective efforts of the owner and her friends, people who gave their time and whatever skills they had to the project.

The original builder absconded with Baylor's money and materials. Word went out of her plight, and volunteers appeared, sometimes driving more than sixty miles from Tucson. As well as her friends, there were people interested in adobe. Among those who stepped forward were Tucson ar-

chitect Richard Brittain and design consultant Matts Myhrman. They worked weekends, enduring the summer heat and storms, guiding a somewhat makeshift crew toward a sometimes unclear goal.

The construction was often spontaneous. There were times when the owner returned from out of town to find something entirely new, such as a loft space that her son, Tony Stanley, felt inspired to build or a handmade cottonwood ladder tied with deerskin thongs and propped up against the loft, a gift from her friend Waymond Jones. Contributions were numerous. Kent Johnson carved bird and animal heads into the mesquite banister of a stairway leading to a large loft bed-

room. A bookcase with mesquite posts and saguaro ribs appeared in the hobbitlike office.

The project began in 1980, when the land was purchased, the well drilled, and a used windmill installed. By 1981, walls were going up, vigas were put in place, a loft space was built, and dirt floors were laid. The dirt floors lasted seven years, filling the room with a fine dust that seeped into all the corners, attracting undesirable animals, including scorpions who made their homes in the cracks. At one time, a rare storm dumped so much water in the house that the dirt floors started sprouting grass. Eventually the floors were replaced with concrete that will be covered with Mexican clay tiles.

The first structure built was the ramada, an open, free-standing porch, a place to seek shade and have coffee or gather after a day of hard work. Baylor spent many hours through the different seasons watching the sun play out during the day and the stars open up the sky in the evenings. She wanted to learn as much as possible about the light that permeated the land she chose to live on in order to make the best choices regarding the orientation of the house to the sun.

The kitchen ceiling is adorned with

TOP: AN INTIMATE LIVING SPACE CENTERS ON A CORNER FIREPLACE. A MEXICAN RUG COVERS A LIGHT-COLORED CONCRETE FLOOR. ORIGINALLY THERE WERE DIRT FLOORS, BUT FINE DUST WOULD SEEP INTO ALL THE CORNERS.

BOTTOM: WOOD PLANKS PAINTED WHITE ARE USED FOR INSIDE WALLS IN THE BEDROOM. ANTIQUES AND SECONDHAND PIECES FURNISH THE ROOM.

saguaro ribs, and an adobe banco stretches across one end of the living space. Around the south side of the house is an out-of-plumb wall that needed a buttress, which in turn became part of a rock-walled sleeping porch. Running across that side of the house, the porch is a protected place that catches the summer breezes. More rock walls have grown up, low and snakelike, circumventing the native vegetation before turning into arches that attach to the corners of the

house. They define the west garden and are an effort to keep animals out.

The house is self-sufficient. A small solar panel provides power for two lightbulbs, one in the kitchen and one over the desk. A vintage 7-Up cooler substitutes for a refrigerator, and a small propane camp stove is used in the summer. An antique cookstove helps heat the house in the winter, as does a fireplace in the main living area. The greenhouse, which includes a bathroom area, acts as a passive solar collector. The bathtub, a horse trough painted orange and blue, is heated by a Mexican wood-fired hot-water heater. During times of unbearable summer heat, Baylor constructs a primitive evaporative cooling system by hanging a Mexican lace tablecloth outside the front double door.

She sprinkles the cloth with water around thirty times a day, leaving the door open to catch the breezes. Another effective method of cooling off is a plunge in the outside tub set up on a redwood deck with mosquito netting strung around it to keep the bees away. Creative solutions come from living in a hot desert place without access to modern technology.

To the west is a sitting area with a grand view of the setting sun. A covered porch runs half the area's length and shades the walls from the brutal summer heat. It is an outside reprieve from the weather, with tables and chairs and potted plants. The other half is open, welcoming the evenings and giving warmth from the setting sun at the end of a cool day.

The accommodations are primitive by most standards, relying on simple ingenuity. Baylor created microenvironments that work within the limitations imposed by nature.

TO AVOID THE NEED FOR ELECTRICITY, BYRD BAYLOR INSTALLED TWO SOLAR PANELS TO RUN TWO LIGHTBULBS. IN THE KITCHEN A VINTAGE 7-UP COOLER KEEPS PERISHABLES FRESH. A WOOD-BURNING STOVE IS USED FOR COOKING DURING THE WINTER, AND IN THE SUMMER A SMALL PROPANE CAMP STOVE IS ALL THAT IS NEEDED. A PORCELAIN TABLE FROM MEXICO WORKS FOR INFORMAL MEALS, AND OPEN SHELVING KEEPS KITCHEN DISHES AND UTENSILS IN VIEW. SAGUARO RIBS COVER THE KITCHEN CEILING.

PERRY PALACE

When the tenants finally moved out of John McNulty and Jeffrey Brown's newly purchased adobe dream house in Tucson, they took all the bathroom fixtures and the cooler with them, broke every window in the house, and left only their trash.

The house, now called Perry Palace after the street (Perry Avenue), was a boarding-house for people who worked on the rail-road during the 1940s and 1950s. By the 1960s the area had started to run down, and Miss Pitt's Boarding House became a gambling hall. From there it continued on a downward roll until John McNulty, a working potter and ceramics instructor, and Jef-frey Brown, a landscape architect, took over the site and dedicated much of their time and money to the project.

They began by returning the house to its original state, working on one wing until the space was livable, moving in, then working on the rest of the structure, repairing walls, rewiring, reroofing, replastering, painting, planting, and cleaning up loads of trash.

An initial catastrophe did slow things down considerably. Someone tugged on a board that was attached to the tower structure, and suddenly the whole tower started to move and then collapsed. It was rebuilt with twenty-seven hundred adobes made on the site, some of which were reconstituted from the old adobes. The lower portion of the tower is now the guest quarters and bathroom, while the upper portion has a sleeping porch and sitting area.

The house is shielded from the alley by a high wall plastered with white cement mixed with iron oxide as a colorant. A turquoise gate opens onto a landscaped patio highlighting the garden and a front porch. A vintage front door leads into the zaguan, used as a gallery space that connects the front of the house with the rear patio.

Inside, unusual color choices create unexpected relationships that work well with an assortment of eclectic furnishings. In the entry, whitewashed fir planks cover the floor, and overlapping laths painted in metallic gold are used on the ceiling. The walls are a rag-rolled olive green overlaid with a cream varnish. The living room colors are more subdued, with vintage pieces that include Baroque and Art Deco furnishings. Dark turquoise walls with white trim are used in the sitting room and bedroom.

The kitchen is the social hub of the house, the center for activities and gatherings. A large space, the room has turquoise walls washed with spotlighting and covered with framed orange-crate labels and floral and botanical prints. A counter divides the eating area from the work space. Collections

of pottery, wooden folk art, tins, glassware, and other artwork decorate the mantel and masonry hearth of a large adobe fireplace built into one corner. The fireplace is the

source of heat for the kitchen. Benches surround a long wooden table that is covered with a 1950s tablecloth.

Patios ring the house, and bamboo fencing and masonry walls screen the private living spaces from the neighborhood. An old tamarisk tree leans over one side of the house, shading a portion of the yard. Flamingos and a white plaster statue of the Madonna are mixed in with bedding plants and potted flowers that add bright spots of color.

French doors connect the inside to the outside, doubling the living space and tying the patios into the central living section. The patios are decorated similarly to the house, with outside lighting, tables and chairs, wall hangings, sculptures, knickknacks, and even an outside shower and spa.

A newly built studio lies just beyond the main house. John McNulty covets this work space that he shares with Jeffrey Brown. Before it was built John used his front porch as his studio space. Again, the studio opens onto a patio that extends the active work area, a place where there's both indoor and outdoor relationships that utilize Tucson's mild climate.

LA CASITA DE MARIA

LEFT: NATIVE PLANTS GROW AROUND THE ORIGINAL ENTRANCE TO THE COURTYARD OF THE FRIEDERS' HOUSE. THE COMPOUND IS MADE UP OF THREE SEPARATE BUILDINGS ATTACHED TO PATIOS DESIGNED FOR OUTDOOR LIVING. LARGE DESERT TREES ARE PLANTED NEXT TO OUTSIDE WALLS AND IN THE COURTYARD TO SHADE THE HOUSE FROM THE SUMMER SUN. A LUSH DESERT LANDSCAPE OF TALL SAGUAROS, AGAVES, CREOSOTE, BUSHES, OCOTILLOS, PALOVERDE TREES, MESQUITE TREES, CHOLLAS, AND PRICKLY PEARS, SECLUDE THE HOUSE FROM THE STREET.

RIGHT: AN EXTERIOR STAIRWAY LEADS TO A SUNDECK ABOVE THE GUEST HOUSE WITH SPECTACULAR VIEWS OF THE MOUNTAINS AND SURROUNDING AREA.

When Bill Frieder and his family relocated to the Phoenix area from Michigan, his wife, Jan, scoured the area in search of an old home with character, a place that was in harmony with their new desert environment. She eventually stumbled onto La Casita de Maria, an adobe compound of three separate structures surrounding a courtyard ringed by native desert growth. The house needed major repairs, but Jan Frieder saw beyond the walls. "I fell in love with the house when I first looked out from the courtyard and saw Praying Monk on Camelback Mountain. There was also something so peaceful inside the gates. It was a quiet peace that made me feel comfortable."

The Frieders employed Phoenix architect John Douglas, who believes that houses should not be viewed as museums or artifacts but "should be approached as a living process." The working team also included landscape architect Christine Ten Eyck, builder Jon Kitchell, and interior designer Nancy Kitchell.

From the street, a long narrow drive covered with crushed granite moves through a lush desert landscape that includes jojoba, agaves, desert flowers, prickly pears, saguaros, mesquites, paloverdes, and other native plants. Large-canopied trees grow close to the courtyard walls, creating shade from the desert's burning sun. Most of the

WINDOWSILLS ARE EXPOSED
CONCRETE, AND EXTERIOR WALLS
ARE HAND-APPLIED DYED
PLASTER. WOOD-CASEMENT
WINDOWS WERE CAREFULLY
MATCHED AND PAINTED A DEEP
BLUE TO COMPLEMENT THE
ADOBE WALLS. LOW-WATER-USE
PLANTS, EMPLOYED AS ARCHI-
TECTURAL ELEMENTS, CONNECT
THE DIFFERENT AREAS OF THE
COURTYARD. THE GUEST HOUSE
HAS AN INTIMATE PATIO THAT
OPENS UP TO THE MAIN
COURTYARD.

trees look as if they have always been there, but in fact they are recent transplants. Christine Ten Eyck saved full-grown desert trees from the impending doom of an Army Corps of Engineers drainage-canal project in the Phoenix area. A crane and boxes that measured eight by eight by eight feet brought the trees to their present location.

Inside the walls of the courtyard the gardens are given more definition with large sculptured shade trees. Included are five paloverdes and two ironwood trees, which were lifted over the walls with cranes and planted in designated locations, and high-climbing Burbank prickly pear cacti, which line a back wall. Low-water-use plants, employed as architectural elements, connect the different areas of the courtyard. A small fountain with a stone base sits in the middle of the yard. Flower beds are planted with native wildflowers. "The idea was to let the

garden mimic the simplicity of the house," says Christine Ten Eyck. Several patios, all of which are used on a regular basis, were constructed around the house for different functions. When there are just a few people for dinner, they may gather in the more intimate dining area on the pool patio. The center patio works well for large gatherings or even a quiet evening at home.

The exterior walls are a soft earthy brown with blue trim around the door and window frames — colors that don't overpower the landscape, but work with it to form a single cohesive unit. Inside the south building is the heart of the house, where the kitchen and breakfast room open onto the courtyard.

Jan Frieder's insistence on making the size of the rooms conform to the original scale of the house, as well as imitating the informal architecture that once existed, kept the project on track. John Douglas and Jon Kitchell worked together to re-create the feeling of the old house. Jon Kitchell made a special effort to replicate window trim, resurrecting the concrete windowsills and building new ones to match. Fixtures were saved and restored, and Jon Kitchell tried to replace what couldn't be saved by search-

BUILT IN THE 1920S, THE HOUSE REQUIRED CAREFUL RENOVATION TO RETAIN THE ORIGINAL SPIRIT OF THE ARCHITECTURE. ROOM SIZES AND BUILDING MATERIALS WERE KEPT THE SAME. THE LIVING ROOM CEILING WAS REPLACED WITH A DUPLICATE OF THE ORIGINAL. FURNITURE WAS COVERED WITH NATURAL-COTTON FABRICS THAT COMPLEMENT THE EXPOSED ADOBE WALLS WASHED IN WHITE.

ing salvage yards for items that would be appropriate for a 1920s house. A woodworking shop was set up on the site, and skilled craftsmen were hired to do the work.

Nancy Kitchell worked with her clients to furnish the house with simple pieces that would convey an informal feeling and enhance the furnishings that the Frieders already had. In the living room, furniture was covered with natural-cotton fabrics that complement the exposed adobe walls. The inside walls were left unplastered to add texture but were painted white to keep the rooms light. The white walls in the bedroom contribute to its airy atmosphere, adding texture at the same time. As in the rest of the house, simple furnishings fill the room, which is dominated by a steel-frame bed with white bedcovers and pillows. The wooden lintels remained natural. Jan Frieder's tastes are directly connected to her passions. "I avoid things that aren't natural, that are artificial. I like the fabrics around me to be real, especially cotton." Thus evolved the theme for decorating the house.

HOUSE OF MANY PATIOS

LEFT: NEXT TO AN OUTSIDE DOOR WITH A SAGUARO-RIB INSERT IS A POTTED NIGHT-BLOOMING CEREUS THAT ECHOES THE VERTICAL LINES OF THE ARCHITECTURE AT THE THOMASSON HOUSE IN TUCSON.

RIGHT: THE STAGGERED ELEVATIONS AND SOFT-EDGED RECTANGULAR SHAPES, CAUSED BY THE NATURE OF THE MATERIAL, PRODUCE AN ORGANIC ARCHITECTURE THAT HARMONIZES WITH THE ENVIRONMENT.

In the middle of a mesquite thicket on the east side of Tucson is the house of James and Sheryl Thomasson. Built from adobe blocks stabilized with cement and coated with a fine-finish plaster the color of the earth, the walls ease into the landscape without interrupting the setting. Patios open out on every side to create a strong connection between the interior and exterior spaces — hence the name House of Many Patios.

The Thomassons were interested in building a place to live that worked well within the strict limitations of the desert; with the expertise of architect Robert Barnes, they carefully picked elements that combined to create an environmentally appropriate house in a climate that can often be uncomfortable.

Twenty inches of adobe provide a wall thickness that stabilizes the interior temperature of the house, and by mixing marble dust into the final coat of exterior plaster, the Thomassons have managed to create a reflective wall surface. Oversize south-facing windows are used for heat gain in the winter. In the summer, when the sun passes directly overhead, the house is cooled by an underground evaporative cooling system that enters at floor level and pushes the hot air up and out of operable window vents located above. In the living room a fireplace

with a fresh-air vent keeps this end of the house warm. A corner fireplace and high windows help winterize the master bedroom. Thermal-pane windows are used on the north side of the house to minimize temperature extremes. A tapered foam roof over a flat ceiling is protected by rigid insulation that is covered over with a built-up hot roof and sealed with a layer of Cool Coat.

All the rooms in the house except the bathrooms are designed around an enclosed atrium that has an eighteen-foot-high ceiling and resembles a cooling tower in North Africa. High on the south wall of the atrium are operable clerestory windows used along with a centrally located ceiling fan for ventilation during the summer.

The layout of the house is simple. At the front entrance a pair of wooden doors — carved with the ancient Indian flute player, Kokopelli — opens onto a stepped-up foyer that overlooks the living room. Carved corbels and sandblasted fir beams span the twelve-foot-high ceiling. A masonry banco capped with flagstone wraps around the fireplace and underneath a large picture window. Two double doors lead to a brick-paved outdoor sitting area that merges with a cov-

ABOVE: THE LIVING ROOM, A LARGE OPEN SPACE WITH BRICK-ON-SAND FLOORS LAID IN A HERRINGBONE PATTERN, OPENS TO THE OUTSIDE PATIO BY TWO DOUBLE DOORS. THE FURNISHINGS ARE INFORMAL. THE SOFA AND CHAIRS ARE UPHOLSTERED IN COTTON CORDUROY, AND THE COFFEE TABLE IS A MANZANITA ROOT COVERED WITH A GLASS TOP.

PRECEDING PAGES: ADOBE WALLS EASE INTO A LANDSCAPE OF MESQUITE TREES AND NATIVE GROWTH. FLOWERS, WHOSE SEEDS ARE SCATTERED AROUND THE PROPERTY ANNUALLY, ADD COLOR.

LEFT: Because of its ability to withstand the brutal summer heat, steel-framed patio furniture works well for outdoor dining and entertainment.

RIGHT: Flagstone slabs create a half circle around the outdoor Jacuzzi. The other half is bordered by beds of plants and smooth stones.

ered dining patio. Other outside areas, in the front and to the west, have low rounded walls the color of the house separating actively maintained gardens from natural spaces.

A patio on the north side has an outdoor Jacuzzi set into the garden. Urns splash water over the edge and into the pool, and flower beds around the perimeter enliven the space with color. Each room and patio opens up to the next, creating continuity.

A doorway off this patio enters the master bedroom, where long, high windows capture the views to the south and east. Corner wall sconces bathe the room in a soft light that can be supplemented by reading lamps next to the bed. While finishing construc-

tion of the room, one of the plasterers sculpted a serpent on the wall in a moment of congenial artistic inspiration. When Sheryl Thomasson saw the slithering reptile, she asked if the plasterer would do other animals in different areas. The house now has a collection of its own desert inhabitants.

The wall color is the same throughout the house: a pale sandstone made by taking a standard light peach paint and mixing it with the same amount of white paint, producing a comfortable nonglare tone.

Outside, the elevation is made up of soft-edged rectangular shapes that generate forms compatible with the land. By nature, adobe produces uneven wall surfaces, which bothered the builder, but delighted the Thomassons, who have always enjoyed the irregular wall surfaces of adobe houses. By using both ancient and contemporary solutions as well as materials indigenous to the site, they are living in a structure that responds well to the forces of nature.

ART AS ARCHITECTURE

LEFT: BRIGHTLY PAINTED MEXICAN HANDCRAFTED PIECES FURNISH THE SIDE PATIO AT THE KEMP HOUSE, NORTH OF PHOENIX.

RIGHT: WELL-PLACED WINDOWS FRAME SELECTED VIEWS OF THE LANDSCAPE.

I n Adobes de la Tierra, an area that is part of the Sonoran Desert and north of Phoenix, artist William Tull designed a residence for the Kemp family that goes beyond the scope of ordinary architecture. He used soft and pliable unfired adobe as his medium and allowed the natural rock forms crowning the building site to dictate the shape of the house. As a result, the boulder-strewn landscape was integrated directly into the design, effectively camouflaging many of the man-made elements. The undulating contours of the granite rocks determined the elevations of the walls as well, which appear as layers of soft shapes mimicking the landscape. It is a spectacular residence that not only relates harmoniously to its environment, but also functions as organic sculpture.

Low, stepped-down adobe walls, irregular and wavering, and a narrow drive, covered with crushed granite to hold down the desert dust, which builds until the heavy July and August rains, signal the approach to the house. The structure rests on property crowded not only with boulders but with native vegetation such as mesquites, paloverdes, saguaros, canyon ragweed, creosote bushes, and triangle-leaf bursages. A wet winter season brings a lavish display of wildflowers in the spring. Delicate yellow flowers cover the paloverde trees, penstemmon

LEFT: BECAUSE OF ITS ROUNDED CORNERS AND ODD-ANGLED PARAPETS, THE HOUSE INTEGRATES WELL WITH THE LANDSCAPE. WILLIAM TULL DESIGNED THE HOUSE AROUND THE BOULDER-STREWN TERRAIN.

TOP: THE DESIGNER TOOK ADVANTAGE OF THE SITE'S ROCK FORMATIONS BY INCORPORATING THE HUGE BOULDERS DIRECTLY INTO THE WALLS.

MIDDLE: OUTDOOR FIREPLACES MAKE PATIOS USABLE EVEN ON COLD WINTER DAYS OR COOL EVENINGS.

BOTTOM: ADOBE WALLS SEEM TO TAKE ON A CERTAIN FLUIDITY, WORKING THEIR WAY AROUND GRANITE BOULDERS. AN OUTDOOR FIREPLACE HEATS THE SITTING AREA ON THE WEST PATIO OFF THE GREAT ROOM.

TOP: A HANDCRAFTED WOOD-
AND-IRON CHANDELIER HANGS
FROM THE CENTER OF A SMALL
DOME IN THE DINING AREA. THE
DINING ROOM TABLE IS A THICK
SLAB OF WALNUT. THE CHAIRS
ARE COVERED WITH HAND-
PAINTED LINEN FABRIC.

BOTTOM: SAGUARO-RIB
SHUTTERS HELP CONTROL THE
HEAT. WHEN CLOSED, THEY LET
IN NARROW, VERTICAL BANDS OF
LIGHT.

bloom in rich shades of pink and red, and the white flowers of saguaro open to the bats for pollination.

The exterior adobe walls, an earthy sand color, blend discreetly with the setting, and their rounded corners and odd-angled parapets, reminiscent of Moroccan Kasbahs south of the Atlas Mountains, suggest a link to much older desert architecture.

A curving flagstone stairway, flanked on one side with granite boulders, leads to the patio and front entrance where the Kemp home already feels like an oasis. A breeze elicits soothing notes from a wind chime in a paloverde tree, while the refreshing sound of water splashing over rock comes from a small waterfall as it empties into a pool on the front patio. The flagstone continues

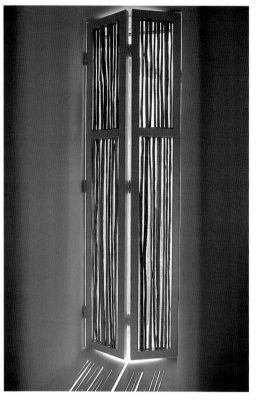

seamlessly into the house, where, just inside the main entry, a large boulder seems to grow out of the earth and architecture. A glass window, cut to fit around the rock and extending up to the beamed ceiling, further blurs the distinction between interior and exterior spaces.

Throughout the house, picture windows

and glass doors frame views of the desert to the east and west. Morning and evening light fills the rooms and provides welcome warmth during the cooler winter months. On warm days ceiling fans keep the air moving, and the house is opened up for cross-ventilation. Saguaro-rib shutters also control the heat. Ceilings are high, but vary from room to room; walls are smooth plaster and light in color. Everywhere there are openings of odd heights and dimensions, asymmetrical by design.

Through an arched entryway is the kitchen, a large square space with a center island and cabinets designed by Tull. All edges are softened, as is the case throughout the house, be it a cabinet, a hood above the stove, or a wall. Within the kitchen is an

eating area that can be warmed by a fireplace. There are nine fireplaces within the boundaries of the property.

In the main living space, or great room, an overhead dome with prismatic glass scatters outside light around the room. The space is divided into two sitting areas, each with a fireplace, and more boulders have been incorporated into the room's design. A large picture window and glass doors look to the west, where adobe and rock form the "sunset deck." In this outdoor living area, a fireplace and built-in banco are surrounded by low walls and spectacular views.

On the other side of the house, a double door closes off the master suite from the rest of the rooms. The beams are especially attractive, hand-hewn with a drawknife. Another focal point of the master suite is a stairway between the south wall and a line of boulders that lead to an outside path and the Jacuzzi. The pool area is also designed to be part of the natural surroundings. The entire compound, both interior and exterior, forms a harmonious relationship with the land — the approach that Tull believes is essential when designing in a fragile environment.

THE GREAT ROOM HAS TWO SITTING AREAS, ONE FOR VIEWING TELEVISION AND THE OTHER FOR ENTERTAINING. EACH AREA CENTERS ON A FIREPLACE. THE CONVERSATION AREA LOOKS OUT ONTO THE WEST PATIO, WITH VIEWS OF THE SURROUNDING LANDSCAPE. THE CHAIRS AND SOFA ARE UPHOLSTERED IN HEAVY OFF-WHITE CHENILLE. A TWO GREY HILLS NAVAJO RUG LIES UNDER A MARBLE COFFEE TABLE WITH IRON LEGS. BETWEEN TWO ARMCHAIRS IS AN ANCIENT WOODEN GRANARY BIN FROM MEXICO.

ROUNDED SHAPES AND SOFT
EDGES ARE USED ON WINDOWS,
WALLS, AND DOOR OPENINGS,
BRINGING TO MIND THE
ARCHITECTURE OF NORTH
AFRICA.

CALIFORNIA

In southern California, yuccas and creosote bushes rise out of the flat stretches of the lower Colorado Desert, a subdivision of the Sonoran Desert. Joshua trees spread their gangly limbs across the Mojave Desert. From Arizona and Nevada, a few fingers of the Great Basin Desert inch over the California border. There are more than thirty-nine thousand square miles of desert in California. Rocky mountains shoot upward from the desert floor, and granite boulders are strewn around haphazardly. Hidden springs support clusters of tall palms and a healthy population of wildlife, but rainfall is scarce. The southern coastline has even less rainfall than parts of the Sonoran Desert. Only through miles of pipelines carrying water to agricultural lands and urban areas can southern California sustain its productivity and population.

In 1768, Spain assigned Father Junipero Serra, a Franciscan priest, the task of planning the colonization of California, which was to include the establishment of missions, presidios, and pueblos. Nine in the long line of missions that reaches from San Diego to San Francisco were founded by the energetic priest. Influenced by Spanish architecture, they were built of adobe or stone and had large enclosed courtyards and long colonnades. Roofs were thatched, but as these were often destroyed by fire (from the burning arrows of native tribes), they were later replaced by the clay tiles that are so characteristic

ABOVE: THE SERRA CHAPEL AT THE MISSION SAN JUAN CAPISTRANO IS THE OLDEST BUILDING IN CALIFORNIA. THE ADOBE CHAPEL WAS FINISHED IN 1777 UNDER THE GUIDANCE OF FATHER JUNIPERO SERRA, FOUNDER OF NINE MISSIONS IN CALIFORNIA. IN 1922, FATHER O'SULLIVAN BEGAN RESTORATION OF THE CHAPEL, BEING CAREFUL TO INCORPORATE AS MUCH OF THE ORIGINAL MATERIAL AS POSSIBLE.

LEFT: THE MOJAVE DESERT IN CALIFORNIA IS AN INTERMEDIATE ZONE BETWEEN THE SONORAN AND THE GREAT BASIN DESERTS, WITH CHARACTERISTICS OF BOTH, INCLUDING VAST EXPANSES OF CREOSOTE BUSHES AND SHADSCALES. THE GANGLY-LIMBED JOSHUA TREE IS ALSO FOUND HERE. THE TURTLE MOUNTAINS RISE OUT OF THE DESERT FLOOR, SLICED BY CANYONS THAT HAVE POCKETS OF PALM TREES AND FRESHWATER SPRINGS.

PRECEDING PAGES: BUILT IN 1936 BY WILLIAM KIRCHNER, A TILE MANUFACTURER, THIS SPANISH ECLECTIC–STYLE HOUSE IN PALM SPRINGS FORMS A U SHAPE, WHICH WRAPS AROUND A REFLECTING POOL AND FACES THE SAN JACINTO MOUNTAINS.

of the Spanish Colonial Revival architecture of today.

Less than a century later, the American overland movement to California was pioneered by trapper and guide Jedediah Smith. By the 1840s, hundreds of settlers had come to California. John C. Frémont arrived in California in 1843, guided by Kit Carson. Frémont surveyed, charted, and produced maps showing the trails of the trappers in the western territory and publicized their routes, bringing more people from the East to the West.

Then, in 1846, acting under orders from President Polk, Commodore Sloat landed with 250 marines and seamen in Monterey and hoisted the United States flag. American naval forces subsequently entered Los Angeles and raised their flag without opposition until Captain Stockton began inciting hostility among the local Mexican population. Hundreds rose up in retaliation, and anti-American sentiment spread. In December, General Kearny, coming to California from Kansas, encountered 150 Californians, under the leadership of Andres Pico, encamped at an Indian village near present-day Escondido. The resulting battle left 22 of Kearny's men dead, and the war with Mexico was officially under way. It was not until the signing of the Treaty of Guadalupe Hidalgo that the war ended, on February 2, 1848, the same year James Wilson Marshall discovered gold while he was employed at Sutter's

ABOVE: IN PALM SPRINGS, A SPANISH ECLECTIC–STYLE HOUSE WITH A MISSION TILE ROOF HAS LARGE SHADE TREES AROUND ITS PERIMETER TO LOWER THE TEMPERATURE. NATIVE PLANTS ARE MIXED WITH FORMAL GARDEN ELEMENTS. SAGUAROS, SOTOLS, GOLDEN BARRELS, AND AGAVES FORM AN OASIS OF GREEN. ALTHOUGH THE HOUSE WAS RECENTLY RENOVATED BY BUD AND BARBARA HOOVER, THE ORIGINAL CHARACTER REMAINS INTACT.

LEFT: WITHOUT OBSTRUCTING THE VIEW, A LOW WALL HELPS DEFINE A PRIVATE BACKYARD SPACE FROM THE OPEN DESERT IN BORREGO SPRINGS.

Mill. Within months, 2,000 men were in the area digging for gold, and by the end of 1849 115,000 settlers were living in California. In 1850 California gained its statehood.

The building of the railroad further increased the numbers that moved west. With the rise in population came the focus on water. By the early 1900s the federal government had started building dams to service the growing agricultural interests and rising number of people. Groundwater was be-

ing depleted at an accelerated rate and needed to be supplemented by surface water, at least in the eyes of the growers. But water projects brought even more land into production. Instead of relieving the overdraft of well water, the water projects only increased the problem.

Southern California would still be a vast wasteland were it not for diversions from the Owens Valley Project, the Colorado River, and northern California, and the immeasurable amounts of water pumped from below the earth's surface, supporting the state's ever-growing population and needs.

RANCHO SANTA FE

In 1906, the Santa Fe Railway purchased a large tract of real estate in southern California, including the historic Osuna estate. The company planned to plant and grow eucalyptus trees for future use as railroad ties, a project that had worked well in Australia. Unfortunately, the variety of eucalyptus that grew in California was too soft, and by 1916 the plan went defunct, leaving the company with six thousand acres of land along the San Dieguito River. The company decided to capitalize on the land by way of real estate development, which meant they needed to secure a permanent source of water. They formed a partnership with W. G. Henshaw, who had the riparian rights along the San Dieguito River as well as control of the dam sites. The Santa Fe Land Improvement Company, a subsidiary of the railroad, hired the architectural firm Requa and Jackson, which assigned the project to architect Lillian Rice, one of the few women architects of her time.

This was a period in California's history when missions were romanticized, spawning architecture influenced by the Islamic the Middle East and southern Spain, including the Mission Revival and Spanish Colonial Revival architectural styles. It was from the Spanish Colonial Revival that Rice drew her inspiration and designs for Rancho Santa Fe, using long, rambling walls with red tiled

roofs and simple lines highlighted by carved-wood corbels and exterior balconies.

Several years ago, Jim Stoltzfus, a retired businessman, and his companion, Floyd Humphreys, an interior designer from the East Coast, purchased a home in Rancho Santa Fe designed by Rice with the intention of restoring the residence, which had been altered over the years, to its original form. Doors and windows needed to be replaced, cracked plaster repaired, and many interior walls from previous remodeling removed. They found craftsmen in Mexico who could duplicate the hardware and lighting fixtures of the 1920s. Fireplaces were replastered inside and out. The size of some windows was increased to bring more of the outside in, but the tiled windowsills and clay-tile floors were left in place.

In landscaping, the owners took advantage of the natural topography, as Rice, a believer in the integration of landscape and architecture, would have done — redefining walkways that lead to the different levels of the garden and to the various buildings on the property. Although brown and dry rolling hills can be seen in the distance (rainfall in Rancho Santa Fe is only eight to ten inches a year), the property has been transformed into a lush oasis. Flagstone paths and

THE U-SHAPED HOUSE WRAPS AROUND A FRONT COURTYARD THAT IS PAVED WITH WORN BRICKS. THE SPREADING LIMBS OF AN OLD OLIVE TREE SHADE MOST OF THE PATIO.

TOP: WHERE REPLACEMENTS WERE NEEDED, COPIES WERE MADE TO MATCH THE ORIGINAL LIGHTING FIXTURES IN THE LIVING ROOM. THE FIREPLACES WERE REWORKED, AND THE WALLS WERE REPLASTERED. THE CORNER PIECE WAS CUSTOM-BUILT AROUND A PAIR OF SPANISH COLONIAL DOORS, AND THE COFFEE TABLE IS AN OLD MEXICAN DOOR. CLAY TILES COVER THE FLOOR.

MIDDLE: THE LINK BETWEEN THE TWO WINGS OF THE HOUSE IS THE FOYER, WHICH HAS MINIMAL FURNISHINGS, KEEPING THE SPACES OPEN.

BOTTOM: FLAGSTONE FLOORING COVERS THE DINING ROOM, SITTING AREA, AND KITCHEN. THE REFECTORY TABLE WAS DESIGNED BY FLOYD HUMPHREYS TO FIT THE SPACE. THE MEXICAN WEDDING CHEST ON THE LEFT DATES FROM 1707.

steps wind their way past sitting areas, narrow channels spill water over rocks into pools, and gardens are filled with succulents and flowers. A Eugenia hedge with cutout

arches encircles an intimate cutting garden with a small sitting area. There are also meditation areas, a pool, and porches.

Certain sacrifices had to be made in order to keep the historical plan intact. The general layout remains the same as it was in the 1920s, with the house nestled into the landscape on the north while the south opens up to the countryside. Rice was known for her low, rambling country houses that did not overpower a setting. Any addition to the exterior would have destroyed the flow and style of the house, so Stoltzfus and Humphreys left the outer walls untouched.

The main house is simple and direct. The U-shape encloses a front courtyard, which has a gated entry and is paved with worn bricks and shaded by the spreading limbs of an old olive tree. The refreshing sound of bubbling water comes from a fountain against one wall. The white surfaces of the house provide a break between the texture and color of the red clay roof tiles and the brick pavers. In the two-story bedroom wing a balcony with a wrought-iron railing — an architectural feature reminiscent of Spain — looks out past the courtyard to the north.

Tucked into one corner of the first floor is an informal glass-and-wrought-iron door used for the main entrance. A small foyer opens up to the living room, a large space

An oasis or a sanctuary was created on the south patio. Lounging and sitting areas surround the odd-angled pool. Potted plants and beds of flowers provide pockets of color.

with two fireplaces — one in the center and the other at the far end. Dark square-cut beams span the width of the ceiling, and clay tiles and area rugs cover the floor. A custom-made double door with screens leads to a covered patio with a circular banco built around a masonry table. Vines hang down over the roofline, shading one side of the patio from the morning sun. The other side faces south, where the sun pours in during the winter months.

Throughout the house windows and doors are left open, allowing soft breezes to ventilate the house without a backup cooling system. On winter evenings, the house is closed and heated by fireplaces.

The interior furnishings are pieces that work well with the architecture. An antique wedding chest from old Mexico is in the dining room. The dining table, custom-built for the space, is a copy of a refectory table. On one windowsill sits a coiled Anasazi pot.

PUMPKIN HOUSE

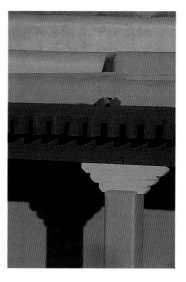

The town of Borrego Springs is located in the Borrego Valley, surrounded by mountain ranges and lean desert scrub. Not far from the center of town, past palm groves and colorful wildflowers, is the entrance to Rams Hill, an exclusive residential area marked by stone walls, flowering brittlebushes, and bedding plants. A narrow blacktop road winds past new houses and native vegetation until the Pumpkin House, named for its terra-cotta walls, emerges from the countryside.

The house is owned by Maurice and Charmaine Kaplan. Charmaine Kaplan, a native Californian from San Diego, says, "It was flight from the city that brought us here. Borrego Springs is literally the last frontier. We feel that the town's limited development is its greatest attraction."

With rounded corners instead of sharp angles, the house reflects the way the Kaplans view desert living — open and inviting. Porches and pairs of French doors allow the interior to stretch outside, creating open living spaces with smooth transitions between the house and the native landscape.

The front of the property is terraced, its levels mirroring the adjacent terrain with its native rocks and vegetation, including ocotillos, paloverdes, yuccas, saguaros, barrel cacti, and desert marigolds. Posts and cor-

bels support a covered walkway leading up to the front entrance, where turquoise doors open onto the foyer. Off to one side is a front porch, entered from the dining room. Protected from the hot southwestern breezes, it is warmed by the mild morning sun and is a sheltered retreat from the natural elements.

Three double doors on the south end of the living area open onto the back porch, bathed in natural light by several skylights. Teakwood furniture and an outdoor couch with overstuffed pillows and cushions are often used in the evenings or on a chilly afternoon. Beyond the porch, on the south side of the house, a sunken fireplace spirals upward and is bordered by desert plants on one side and a semicircular banco on the other.

ABOVE: A SUNKEN CONVERSATION AREA SURROUNDS A SPIRAL FIREPLACE ON THE SOUTH SIDE OF THE HOUSE.

RIGHT: THERE IS AN EASY TRANSITION BETWEEN THE DESERT LANDSCAPE AROUND BORREGO SPRINGS AND THE EDGES OF THE HOUSE. THE ORANGE COLOR OF THE OUTSIDE WALLS GAVE THE PUMPKIN HOUSE ITS NAME.

TOP: THE GUEST HOUSE EAST OF THE POOL AREA IS WARM AND SUNNY DURING THE WINTER MONTHS.

BOTTOM: A LARGE FIREPLACE IS THE FOCAL POINT OF THE SEATING AREA IN THE LIVING ROOM. THE ROOF SUPPORTS ARE MASSIVE BEAMS, WITH DIAGONAL CEDAR STRIPS WASHED WITH A LIGHT STAIN BETWEEN THEM. A NAVAJO RUG, COCHITI DRUM, MEXICAN-TILE FLOOR, AND MEXICAN FURNITURE ADD TO THE RUSTIC CHARM. THREE DOUBLE DOORS OPEN ONTO A COVERED PORCH ON THE SOUTH SIDE.

This area functions as a warm and comfortable outdoor space for entertaining.

After spending some time in Borrego Springs the Kaplans decided they wanted a pool, but they did not want it to spoil their view or create an eyesore in the desert. The solution was to conceal the pool on an adjacent piece of land, behind walls that blend with the house. On one side of the pool area, they added a guest house with a rooftop pa-

IN THE MASTER BEDROOM FURNISHINGS ARE PART OF THE ARCHITECTURE. MASONRY END TABLES AND THE BED ARE EXTENSIONS OF THE WALLS. ABOVE THE BED, *NICHOS* IN THE WALL HOUSE A COLLECTION OF HOPI KACHINAS MADE BY COOLIDGE ROY AND ALVIN NAVASIE.

tio that is walled in by high parapets, creating an upper-level outdoor room.

Inside the main house, the living room, dining room, and kitchen flow together as one common space, divided only by columns between the living and dining areas, and a kitchen counter that separates the dining area from where the cooking is done. Mexican pavers are used for flooring, and the ceilings are supported by massive beams, with split cedar set on a diagonal between the beams. Wall colors are kept light, and wide shuttered windows control the amount of heat and sun that penetrate the interior.

Centered on the far wall of the living room is a large fireplace. Its plastered hearth extends into a semicircular banco underneath a pair of corner windows, a sitting area with comfortable cushions and pillows. In front of the fireplace is a large Navajo area rug along with other New Mexican furnishings, which not only complement the architecture but also repeat patterns found in the architectural design of the house.

Art and handmade objects can be found throughout the house; the Kaplans believe it is important to live with art in their everyday environment. A Huichol yarn painting that hangs in the foyer depicts a scene of a husband whose unfaithfulness to his wife is avenged by five different plants. In the living room an R. C. Gorman pot becomes part of the decor, and a Cochiti drum doubles as an end table next to a couch. *Nichos* in the bedroom hold art objects ranging from Hopi kachinas to Pai Pai pots from northern Baja.

The layout of the master bedroom is simple. Most of the bedroom furnishings are built in, mere extensions of the plastered walls. A bed platform with side tables and cubbyholes underneath seems to roll out from the wall. Above, recessed lighting casts a pale yellow glow that brings out the room's warm tones in the evening. A pair of French doors can be opened to a front porch, letting in pure white morning light from the northeast and allowing the soft breezes to circulate.

Even the master bathroom has a direct connection to the desert, with long windows opening up to the scenery and a door leading to an outdoor spa where the Kaplans can enjoy the tranquillity of the setting.

LA QUINTA CONTEMPORARY

LEFT: THE BACK PATIO EASILY BECOMES AN EXTENSION OF THE LIVING ROOM. SCRIM CURTAINS CAN BE DRAWN ACROSS RECESSED TRACKING IN THE OUTSIDE OVERHANG, EXPANDING THE SIZE OF THE LIVING ROOM AND ALLOWING THE AIR TO CIRCULATE.

RIGHT: THIS VIEW OF THE SEMIENCLOSED BACK PATIO SHOWS HOW THE SCRIM CURTAINS MAY BE PULLED BACK WHEN NOT IN USE.

FOLLOWING PAGE: ARCHITECT KEN RONCHETTI DESIGNED A WALLED COMPOUND SIMILAR TO THOSE IN NORTH AFRICA, SPAIN, AND MEXICO. POOLS OF WATER HAVE THE EFFECT OF A GIANT EVAPORATIVE COOLING SYSTEM WHEN BREEZES BLOW ACROSS THEM.

In the midst of a jagged mountainous landscape and flatlands filled with creosote bush, dry arroyos, lizards, and jackrabbits is the lush oasis of La Quinta, a town of expansive green lawns, gardens filled with exotic flowers, and golf courses lined with tall palm trees. It is here that Dan and Norma Hayes asked Ken Ronchetti to design their house.

After studying the prevailing winds in both the summer and winter as well as the views, Ronchetti decided to develop a walled compound similar to those in North Africa, Spain, and Mexico, but one that could also open up easily to the exterior.

Ronchetti's philosophy is "to bring an architecture to southern California that responds to the southern part of this hemisphere rather than taking the north to the south — a drought-tolerant architecture where the plantings, the soil, the architecture are all in harmony." The minimalism of the desert appeals to his design sense, as does the challenge of incorporating the entire property into the project, interweaving land and structure.

Reminiscent of Kasbahs in Morocco, blank walls parallel the street, acting as a buffer. The exterior walls have softened corners that appear eroded by time. Discreetly hidden in the middle of two walls is a tall wooden door that opens onto an elegant

TOP AND MIDDLE: TOWERS AND HORIZONTAL PLANES CREATE ELEVATIONS THAT ARE REMINISCENT OF THOSE OF KASBAHS IN MOROCCO.

BOTTOM: GRACEFUL MESQUITE TREES AND VIBRANT FLOWERS SOFTEN THE BLANK WALLS THAT ACT AS A BUFFER BETWEEN THE COMPOUND AND THE STREET.

courtyard landscaped with pools. Sheets of water cascade over the sides to lower levels. Punctuating the corners of the pools are raised planter boxes with tall slender palms surrounded by bright-colored pansies and petunias.

The main house is designed to be an extension of the exterior living spaces. Glass walls slide back into structural walls, turning rooms into spacious ramadas. The outside overhangs have recessed tracking for a heavy scrim curtain that can be drawn around rooms, keeping out insects but still allowing the air to circulate freely. Screened shutters for privacy also slide out from structural walls, letting in muted light and air for ventilation.

The openings in the house help frame the landscape, incorporating external elements into the design of the house. "Because you have the ability to control the structure by moving the walls around, the house can become very transparent, which has a relaxing effect on people," says Ronchetti, who designs homes to take advantage of moonlight as well as sunlight. Effective combinations of light and shadow seem to further erase the lines between the different spaces.

An outdoor dining area is situated off the kitchen. On one side is a closeted barbecue grill, counter, and sink that make food

preparation easy and convenient. When the house is opened to this direction, the amount of entertaining space is greatly expanded.

The layout is based on a central communal area, flanked by bedroom wings that open onto private patios. Use of color is subtle, always allowing the architecture to be the dominant force. Interior furnishings are minimal — most of the furniture is built-in. The recessed lighting, which is hidden in elevated roof levels and inside wall niches, is seductive and can be turned up or down with dimmer switches. Even the center living room table uses indirect light from lanterns that serve as the base for an etched piece of glass. The table was created by designer Leslie Bochard, who worked with the

LEFT: A QUARRY IN FRANCE PROVIDED ALL THE STONE FOR THE COUNTERS, FLOORS, AND SHOWERS IN THE MASTER BATHROOM. THE CARPETING IS HIGHLY TEXTURED WITH DIFFERING LIGHT VALUES. GLASS DOORS IN FRONT OF THE JACUZZI OPEN ONTO AN INTIMATE WALLED GARDEN WITH FLOWERS AND SEGO PALMS.

RIGHT: THE WEST OPENING IN THE LIVING ROOM FRAMES THE SPECTACULAR DESERT SUNSETS. IN THE CENTER IS A CIRCULAR CONVERSATION AREA WITH OVERSIZE WICKER SEATING UPHOLSTERED WITH LARGE OFF-WHITE CUSHIONS. THE COFFEE TABLE, DESIGNED BY LESLIE BOCHARD, IS MADE FROM A THICK PIECE OF GLASS, WHICH IS DEEPLY ETCHED AND IRREGULAR. THE TOP IS SET ON A BASE OF THREE LIT LANTERNS. IN TWO CORNERS OF THE ROOM, HALF-CIRCLE FIREPLACES ARE USED WHEN TEMPERATURES COOL DOWN. CEILING FANS KEEP THE AIR CIRCULATING.

Ronchetti Design Group and the Hayeses on finding complementary furnishings that would not overpower the architecture.

Fireplaces, ceiling fans, and the house itself are the main sources of heating and cooling. Backup systems are rarely turned on. The degree of heating and cooling is controlled primarily by how opened or closed the rooms are. The patio pools also act as a giant evaporative cooling system fed by the breezes that ripple across the water and through the house.

Graceful mesquite trees dress up a portion of the courtyard next to the guest quarters of the main house. Across the pool, a separate guest house takes up one corner of the patio. Two bedrooms and a central kitchen and eating area can be opened like the main house for light and air, or closed with glass walls or scrim curtains that roll across the overhang for privacy.

Not long ago, the Hayeses were living in Newport Beach, a coastal environment, and Norma Hayes could not imagine living in an inland desert. But today, she can't imagine living anywhere else and believes it is the house that makes living in the desert work so well.

A STAGE FOR DESERT LIGHT

Ricardo Legorreta reached out to the heart of Mexico, a region that has historical connections to both North Africa and southern Spain, to shape an architectural plan to fit the location and needs of his clients Arthur and Audrey Greenberg in Brentwood, California. Audrey Greenberg had always admired the work of Luis Barragán and heard through the UCLA School of Architecture that Ricardo Legorreta worked in similar ways with light, walls, and color. After traveling to Mexico to spend time with the architect, the Greenbergs were convinced that he could design the home that they wanted.

At the Brentwood site, Legorreta took the opportunity to bring back the magic of desert life to Los Angeles, using walls not only as structural elements but as vertical and horizontal components of the landscape. One wall is used as a screen to create privacy, while another opens up to the views and breezes. On the street side, a high-rising front wall gives way to a crushed-rock driveway, the color and texture of the desert.

The movement of the sun is a crucial tool for Legorreta. "I like to have light come from more than one source so there can be different light at different times of the day." Throughout the day, narrow bands of light paint patterns across the front gallery, a transition space between the outer court and the

TOP: THE COMBINATION OF COLORS ON THE WALLS AT DIFFERENT ELEVATIONS RESULTS IN A STRONG UNITY AMONG THEM.

BOTTOM: VERTICAL OPENINGS MAKE USE OF COLOR BETWEEN THEM TO FORM A BOND WITH THE INTERIOR SPACES. LIMESTONE PAVES BOTH THE INSIDE FLOORS AS WELL AS THE OUTSIDE TERRACE AND SEATING AREAS.

living area. In the center core of the house a lavender cooling tower takes in light and breezes and disperses them; at its base is a pool into which water splashes, providing a refreshing sound and sight.

Contrasts of color and intriguing textures abound. Leafy agaves huddle together against the outside front wall, in smooth contrast to the hand-troweled plaster and the stark desert landscape. Inside, the floors are paved with cool slabs of stone.

The living room, which opens to both the front and back galleries, consists of a large space encompassing several intimate conversation areas. Windows are set off-center and at unusual locations, framing areas both inside and out and expanding the space. Legorreta determines where the openings will be according to the views, sometimes putting a window through an interior wall. Spaces contract and then expand, with vibrant color moving the focus from one place to the next. "Color is purely emotional," says Legorreta, "and is a way to create a sense of continuity." An abstract painting hangs above the living room fireplace and echoes the colors and lines of the house. A stairway becomes more than a connection between two points — with a series of linear skylights casting bands of light on the vibrantly colored walls, the stairway is a constantly changing abstract design. Each space in the house has a connection with the next, either with color or shape or texture.

The Greenbergs' back patio is a continuation of the inside. Limestone floors pass through the glass walls to the back terrace and down the steps with uninterrupted movement. Off to the side, a narrow channel of water flows down different levels to pools below, where the water then passes through an open tower with an electric-blue interior. The venetian-blind-like roof of an outdoor room is made with fuchsia strips of metal that cast long shadows against the side walls and continue out to the limestone patio. Underneath, a built-in barbecue is surrounded by a countertop tiled in lemon yellow. Luxurious foliage and terraced beds of flowers on this side of the house connect with the countryside around them, where well-watered gardens extend beyond the horizon line.

Audrey Greenberg says, "There is a sense everywhere of the outdoors being drawn inside. It's also a happy house that is bright, sunny, and colorful — well suited to the southern California climate."

HAWAII

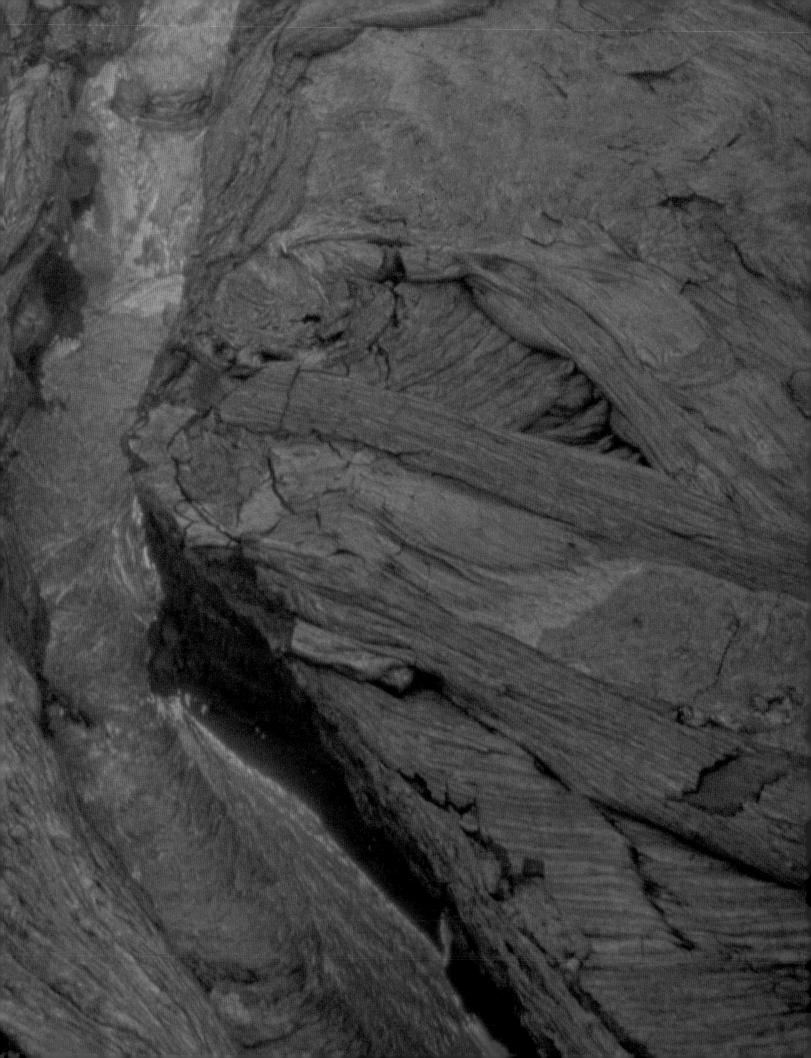

KAHI'IKENAIKALAPIO

LEFT: LARGE OHIA TRUNKS
SUPPORT THE OPEN BEAMS OF
THE SOUTH PATIO. THE POOL,
PROVIDING A COOL RESPITE ON
HOT DAYS, FLOWS INTO A
RETENTION POND, WHICH
ELIMINATES MOST OF THE WATER
LOSS BY CONSTANTLY PUMPING
THE OVERFLOW INTO THE POOL.

RIGHT: BRANCHES FROM THE
OHIA TREE, A NATIVE HARD-
WOOD, CAST DRAMATIC LATE-
AFTERNOON SHADOWS ON THE
PATIO.

PRECEDING PAGES: A RIVER OF
LAVA FLOWS FROM THE VOLCANO
MAUNA LOA (13,680 FEET). THE
RAIN-SHADOW EFFECT OF THIS
VOLCANO AND ITS SISTER,
MAUNA KEA (13,796 FEET),
PRODUCES A DESERT ON THE
DRY, WESTERN SIDE OF THE
MOUNTAIN CHAIN.

The island of Hawaii is still growing through the volcanic activity of Mauna Loa and Kilauea. As pressure builds from below the surface, lava spews forth and flows down the sides of the craters, building up more and more landmass. The third-largest volcano on the island, Hualalai, is dormant but not extinct. Mauna Kea, the white mountain, rising eighteen thousand feet from the ocean floor, and Kohala are both considered inactive, but are actively connected to the mass of molten rock beneath the ocean. The volcanoes are unpredictable and have caused extensive damage in historic times, wiping out whole villages with one engulfing spasm.

On the northwest portion of the island of Hawaii lies a starkly beautiful area. Here the climate is drier than most "true" deserts; total rainfall in some years can be as little as five inches, less than most North American deserts. Occasional brutal winds and storms of flying volcanic dust buffet the unusual location, an arid landscape covered by rolling folds of lava, dry grasses, mesquite and acacia trees, and prickly pear cacti. The island's volcanic mountains rise in the near distance. It is a striking setting for a spectacular contemporary house.

The owners of the house, Jim and Pricilla Growney, chose the site — a narrow spit of an old lava flow — primarily because of its dramatic ocean views. In addition, from their hillside they had a perfect view of a total solar eclipse, including a solar flare, which led to the Hawaiian name they've given their property: Kahi'ikenaikalapio — "the place from which the eclipse was seen." Given the limitations and challenges of the area, namely the powerful winds and fine volcanic soil, the Growneys knew they needed a structure that would function especially well in its environ-ment. They also knew the right designer for the project. They hired Ken Ronchetti, whose work had impressed the Growneys with its simplicity and environmental integrity.

LEFT: THE HOUSE, SET ON LAND FORMED BY AN OLD LAVA FLOW, WAS DESIGNED AS A SERIES OF WIND-CATCHING ARCS THAT ALTERNATELY COLLECT AND REPEL BREEZES.

BELOW: THE MAIN LIVING ROOM HAS VIEWS TO THE SOUTH AND WEST AND IS EASILY TURNED INTO AN OPEN PAVILION. RATTAN FURNITURE, WITH NEUTRAL COTTON AND COLOR-FUL BATIK CUSHIONS, DECO-RATES BOTH THE LIVING ROOM AND SURROUNDING PATIOS.

RIGHT: PETROGLYPHS CARVED INTO LAVA ROCK ILLUSTRATE THAT NATIVE HAWAIIANS AND THEIR ANCESTORS HAVE OCCUPIED THE ISLANDS FOR CENTURIES.

BELOW: THE PATIO AND POOL AREA, BORDERED BY THE LIVING ROOM, DINING ROOM, AND KITCHEN, ARE PROTECTED FROM INTENSE WINDS THAT PERIODICALLY BLOW AGAINST THE FRONT OF THE ARC-SHAPED HOUSE, WHICH IS DESIGNED TO DEFLECT SUCH WINDS.

Ronchetti saw the shape of the land and the sometimes inhospitable demands of the climate as a unique opportunity. He created a central form based on a series of arcs that act like a giant scoop, collecting breezes from the south, while letting the strong north-eastern winds roll off the elliptical shield of the front. Structurally, the house needed to be designed to withstand one-hundred-mile-per-hour winds that can twist, whip, and surge. As a simple solution, transoms and sliding doors became main design elements. When the winds are mild, the house can be

opened on both sides for cross-ventilation. During raging storms, sliding wall panels close off the west end of the house, and the openings can be secured.

A repetition of patterns and materials strengthens the structure's design elements. Flagstone covers the front walk, the house floors, and the southern patio. Custom wooden doors are similar to one another in material and design. An entrance door with narrow horizontal lights rolls back into the wall, erasing the line that normally defines exterior from interior. The foyer, dining room, and living room merge into one large space. Windows in this great room are pairs of doors on raised platforms, with transoms above. The west end of the room extends onto a covered lanai that seemingly floats off into space. The lanai can be closed off from the interior by sliding doors, more than sixteen feet wide and twelve feet high. Around the edge of the lanai, a heavy scrim curtain acts as a privacy screen, still allowing outside air to circulate.

The kitchen connects to the east end of the dining area. It can be closed off from the rest of the house by a set of sliding wooden doors. Although the countertops are the color of volcanic ash, most of the kitchen is a reflective white reminiscent of the interiors of Tunisian mosques. Adjacent to the

kitchen is a curved stairway that leads up to the office and the master bedroom.

The south patio is covered by a grid of open beams, supported by large ohia trunks, a local hardwood similar to ironwood. Between the beams are long straight ohia branches, which serve as a trellis for trailing vines. Beyond the porch is a wading pool, where water cascades over the lowest side into a retention pond below, called a surge pit. The overflow is pumped back into the pool, eliminating most of the water loss.

The exterior and interior designs allow the boundaries of the house to change according to the season or the needs and desires of the owners. When the doors and windows are open the main living space becomes a pavilion. When they are closed, the house becomes a protective shield against the outside elements.

ABOVE: THE HOUSE IS NESTLED IN BUFFALO GRASS, WHERE THE OCCASIONAL ACACIA AND MESQUITE TREE CALL TO MIND THE EXPANSIVE LANDSCAPE OF THE SOUTHWEST.

RIGHT: LARGE DOOR-AND-WINDOW COMBINATIONS OPEN THE LIVING ROOM TO THE PATIOS AND POOL.

SOURCE GUIDE

ARCHITECTS / DESIGNERS / CONTRACTORS / CONSULTANTS

ROBERT E. BARNES, ARCHITECT
9353 N. Casa Grande Hwy.
Tucson, AZ 85743
(520) 744-9268
Structural and thermal analysis for earthern structures and site evaluations.

COBRE BUILDING SYSTEMS
Tim and Diane Putenney
P.O. Box 26587
Tucson, AZ 85726
(520) 882-8010
Custom adobe homes.

JOHN DOUGLAS, ARCHITECT
7522 E. McDonald Dr.
Scottsdale, AZ 85250
(520) 951-2242

HABITAT OF SANTA FE, INC.
D. Perry
947 Camino Santandeer
Santa Fe, NM 87501
(505) 982-3722
Design consultation, furnishings, and accessories.

MICHAEL KINER & ASSOCIATES
73625 Hwy. 111, Suite F
Palm Desert, CA 92260
(619) 773-3390
Specializing in custom homes and historic renovations.

LAKE/FLATO ARCHITECTS, INC.
311 Third St., Suite 200
San Antonio, TX 78205
(210) 227-3335

PAUL LAMB, ARCHITECT
618 Lavaca St., #9
Austin, TX 78701
(512) 478-7316

RICARDO LEGORRETA, ARQUITECTOS
285-A Palacio de Versalles
Mexico City, Mexico 11020
52-5-251-96-98

OUT ON BALE, LTD.
1037 E. Linden St.
Tucson, AZ 85719
(602) 624-1673
Straw-bale consultation and workshops.

RAMMED EARTH DEVELOPMENT
Tom Wuelpern
265 W. 18th St.
Tucson, AZ 85701
(520) 623-2784
fax (520) 623-1219
Designers and builders of fine rammed-earth and adobe homes.

RONCHETTI DESIGN
P.O. Box 474
Rancho Santa Fe, CA 92067
(619) 756-1033
Arid-climate architecture for our time.

SOLAR SURVIVAL ARCHITECTURE
Michael Reynolds
P.O. Box 1041
Taos, NM 87571
(505) 751-0462 or (505) 770-7056 or (505) 770-7057
Earthships.

ROBERT A. STAEHLE, ARCHITECT
P.O. Box 693
Clayton, CA 94517
(510) 672-7726
Western living and custom homes.

STRAWCRAFTERS
Tom Luecke, Owner
3785 Moorhead Ave.
Boulder, CO 80303
(303) 449-1334
fax (303) 499-2508
Design and building service specializing in straw-bale construction, earth plastering methods, poured adobe floors, plus classes and workshops in straw-bale construction.

SURVIVAL HABITAT
P.O. Box 257
Ridgway, CO 81432
(800) SUN-8478
To order information on Earthship construction send or call for list and prices of videos and books available.

TULL COMPANY
W. F. Tull, Designer
5628 N. Scottsdale Rd.
Scottsdale, AZ 85253
(520) 949-0575
fax (520) 970-5805
Adobe homes.

PAUL WEINER, ARCHITECT/BUILDER
Design and Building Consultants
19 E. 15th St.
Tucson, AZ 85701
(520) 792-0873
Specializing in straw, adobe, rammed earth, salvaged metals, concrete, and heavy timbers to create timeless living structures.

TERRY WELANDER CONSTRUCTION
1846 Devon Place,
Vista, CA 92084
(619) 726-9940
Specializing in construction and remodeling.

INTERIOR DESIGN

BOCHARD INTERNATIONAL DESIGN
1128 Ocean Park Blvd., Suite 302
Santa Monica, CA 90405
(310) 858-6634

HABITAT OF SANTA FE, INC.
947 Camino Santander
Santa Fe, NM 87501
(505) 982-3722
Furnishings, accessories, and design.

JAMES P. SAMS, FAC
1143 No. Doheny Dr.
Los Angeles, CA 90069
(310) 247-0740

LANDSCAPE DESIGNERS / SEED SUPPLIERS

ARTERRA (ART OF THE EARTH)
Peter Curé and Michael F. Rockwell, Landscape Architects and Engineering Contractors
2332 E. Quail
Phoenix, AZ 85024
(520) 569-9800
Pools, spas, water features, landscape irrigation, etc. Designers and builders of total outdoor living environments.

JEFFREY BROWN, LANDSCAPE DESIGNER
722 N. Perry
Tucson, AZ 85705
(520) 882-9175

JAMES DAVID, LANDSCAPE ARCHITECT
1818 W. 35th St.
Austin, TX 78703
(512) 451-5490
Garden shop for unusual plants and seeds, sculptural pieces, architectural services, and construction.

CHRISTINE TEN EYCK, LANDSCAPE ARCHITECT
The Planning Center
2525 E. Arizona Biltmore Circle, Suite 236
Phoenix, AZ 85016
(520) 957-2218

GARDEN STONE SUPPLY
2830 Grand Ave.
Phoenix, AZ 85017
(520) 262-9401

MIA LEHRER/SCOTT SEBASTIAN
Landscape Architecture
2227 Talmadge St.
Los Angeles, CA 90027
(213) 664-3419 or (714) 497-4549

BAKER MORROW, LANDSCAPE ARCHITECT
Morrow and Company
210 La Peta NE
Albuquerque, NM 87108
(505) 268-2266

NATIVE SEED SEARCH
2509 N. Campbell, #325
Tucson, AZ 85719
(520) 327-9123
Send $1.00 for catalog.

FURNISHINGS

ACCAZIA DESIGN
1818 W. 35th St.
Austin, TX 78703
(512) 206-0188
Manufacturers of unique wood outdoor furniture.

ADOBE ELEGANCE
Route 3, Box 37
Torrero, NM 87573
(505) 757-2518
Unique clay light fixtures by potter Robin Reindle, created to accent your southwestern decor.

ANTIQUA DE MEXICO
7037 N. Oracle Rd.
Tucson, AZ 85704
(520) 742-7114
fax (520) 575-0576
Custom Mexican Colonial furniture, including wrought iron, as well as folk arts, glassware, pottery, tinware, paintings, and lighting fixtures.

¡AQUÍ ESTÁ!
204 S. Park Ave.
Tucson, AZ 85719
(520) 798-3605
Handcrafted reproductions of Spanish Colonial and traditional Southwest furniture and accessories.

ARTISANS OF THE DESERT
901 3rd St. NW
Albuquerque, NM 87102
(505) 247-9725
Handcrafted furniture, kitchen cabinets, doors, carved beams and corbels.

JANET BURNER
326 E. 5th St.
Tucson, AZ 85705
(520) 624-5201
Architectural ceramic pieces: custom fountains, wall pieces, and miscellaneous.

BUTLER CUSTOM DOORS
12300 E. 5th St.
Tucson, AZ 85748
(520) 885-8305
Distributor for SW Door Co. Also manufacturers of custom doors, including etched glass, inlaid copper, and other custom designs.

COMO NO?
830 Canyon Rd.
Santa Fe, NM 87501
(800) 729-5816
Art and furniture gallery specializing in contemporary and traditional Southwest furnishings.

DESIGNS SOUTHWEST
1803 6th St. NW
Albuquerque, NM 87102
(800) 999-8167
Furnishings, accessories, and design.

BRUCE EICHER, INC.
8755 Melrose Ave.
West Hollywood, CA 90069
(310) 657-4630
Designers and manufacturers of lighting fixtures and iron furniture, also extensive collection of antique Mexican Colonial furniture and reproductions.

EL PASO IMPORT CO.
311 Montana
El Paso, TX 79902
(915) 542-4241
Originals from Mexico: Colonial and ranchero furniture, folk art, ironwork, and architectural pieces.

FIESTA FURNISHINGS
7848 E. Redfield, Suite 11
Scottsdale, AZ 85260
(520) 951-3239
Furnishings from old Mexico.

FORM AND FUNCTION
328 S. Guadalupe St.
Santa Fe, NM 87501
(505) 984-8226
Authentic Southwest lighting. Handcrafted lights from natural materials: iron, clay, glass, etc.

HOLLER AND SANDERS, LTD.
P.O. Box 2151
Nogales, AZ 85628
(520) 287-5153
Antiques and contemporary furniture, stone, pottery, and architectural components.

LA CASA MEXICANA
5855 E. Broadway, #112
Tucson, AZ 85711
(520) 745-9591
fax (520) 745-6939
Custom-made furniture: *equipales*, tile, lamps, accessories.

RONNIE MARTIN
R&D Welding
Route 1, Box 378
Graham, TX 76450
(817) 549-9771
Unique horseshoe and western furniture, custom designed.

JOHN McNULTY
722 N. Perry Ave.
Tucson, AZ 85705
(520) 882-9175
Ceramicware for southwestern living.

SONORAN TRADERS
1515 N. Wilmot Rd.
Tucson, AZ 85712
(520) 722-1548
Handcrafted tribal arts.

SOUTHWEST SPANISH CRAFTSMEN
328 S. Guadalupe
P.O. Box 1805
Santa Fe, NM 87504
(505) 982-1767 or (800) 777-1767
Fine furniture and doors. Catalog $5.00.

BUILDING SUPPLIES

OLD PUEBLO ADOBE CO.
9353 N. Casa Grande Hwy.
Tucson, AZ 85743
(520) 744-9268
Adobe, mortar and plaster mixes, vigas, corbels, latillas, specialty southwestern materials, furnishings.

SOUTHWEST DOOR CO.
219 N. 3rd Ave., Suite 108
Tucson, AZ 85705
(520) 624-1434
Specializing in southwestern-style doors and cabinet fronts in pine, cedar, and mesquite; cedar casement windows; pine and mesquite flooring; and custom door and cabinet hardware.

ORGANIZATIONS

CORNERSTONES
P.O. Box 2341
Santa Fe, NM 87504
(505) 982-9521
Preservation of historical buildings.

NEW MEXICO COMMUNITY FOUNDATION
Grace Jepson, Executive Director
1472½ St. Francis Dr.
Santa Fe, NM 87505
(505) 820-6860
Grant making, convening, and technical assistance with special emphasis on rural communities and rural issues.

B I B L I O G R A P H Y

Adams, Ward R. *History of Arizona.* 4 vols. Phoenix: Record Publishing, 1930.

Austin, Mary. *The Land of Little Rain.* New York: Penguin Books, 1988.

Barnes, F. A. *Canyon Country, Geology for the Layman and Rockhound.* Wasatch Publishers, 1978.

Bender, Gordon L. *Reference Handbook on the Deserts of North America.* Westport, Conn. and London: Greenwood Press, 1982.

Bourgeois, Jean-Louis, and Carollee Pelos. *Spectacular Vernacular.* New York: Aperture Book, 1989.

Bowles, Paul. *Their Heads Are Green and Their Hands Are Blue.* New York: Ecco Press, 1991.

Brown, David E., ed. *Desert Plants, Biotic Communities of the American Southwest-United States and Mexico.* Vol. 4, no. 1–4. Tucson: University of Arizona, for Boyce Thompson Southwestern Arboretum, 1982.

Bunting, Bainbridge. *Early Architecture in New Mexico.* Albuquerque: University of New Mexico Press, 1976.

Carver, Norman F. *Iberian Villages, Portugal and Spain.* Kalamazoo, Mich.: Documan Press, 1988.

———. *North African Villages, Morocco, Algeria, Tunisia.* Kalamazoo, Mich.: Documan Press, 1989.

Chapin, Frederick. *Land of the Cliff Dwellers.* Tucson: University of Arizona Press, 1988.

Cheek, Larry. *Arizona.* Oakland, Calif.: Compass American Guides, 1991.

Chronic, Halka. *Roadside Geology of New Mexico.* Missoula, Mont.: Mountain Press Publishing, 1987.

Clark, Kenneth N., and Patricia Paylore, eds. *Desert Housing.* Tucson: University of Arizona, Office of Arid Land Studies, 1980.

Covey, Cyclone, ed. and trans. *Adventures in the Unknown Interior of America.* Albuquerque: University of New Mexico Press, 1990.

Creswell, K. A. C. *A Short Account of Early Muslim Architecture.* Baltimore, Md.: Penguin Books, 1958.

Crowther, Geoff, and Hugh Finlay. *Morocco, Algeria, and Tunisia: A Travel Survival Kit.* Berkeley, Calif.: Lonely Planet Publications, 1989.

Cummings, Joe. *Texas Handbook.* Chico, Calif.: Moon Publications, 1990.

Day, A. Grove. *Coronado's Quest: The Discovery of the American Southwest.* Honolulu, Hawaii: Mutual Publishing Paperback Series, 1988.

Díaz, Bernal. *The Conquest of New Spain.* Baltimore, Md.: Penguin Books, 1965.

Eisen, Johnathan, and Harold Straughn. *Unknown Texas.* New York: Collier Books, Macmillan, 1988.

Epstein, Sam and Beryl. *All About the Desert.* New York: Random House, 1957.

Fehrenbach, T. R. *Lonestar: A History of Texas and Texans.* New York: Collier Books, Macmillan, 1968.

Ferguson, Erna. *New Mexico.* New York: Alfred A. Knopf, 1951.

———. *Our Southwest.* New York: Alfred A. Knopf, 1952.

Fiero, Bill. *Geology of the Great Basin.* Reno: University of Nevada Press, 1986.

Foster, Lynne. *Adventuring in the California Desert.* San Francisco: Sierra Club Books, 1987.

Foster, Nancy Haston. *The Alamo and Other Texas Missions to Remember.* Houston, Tex.: Gulf Publishing, 1984.

Fradkin, Philip A. *Sagebrush Country: Land and the American West.* New York: Alfred A. Knopf, 1989.

Fugate, Francis L. and Roberta B. *Roadside History of New Mexico.* Missoula, Mont.: Mountain Press Publishing, 1989.

Gilmore, Ray N. and Gladys. *Readings in California History.* New York: Thomas Y. Crowell, 1966.

Gilpin, Laura. *The Rio Grande.* New York: Duell, Sloan, and Pearce, 1949.

Goodwin, Godfrey. *Islamic Spain.* San Francisco: Chronicle Books, 1990.

Grimes, Joel. *Navajo: Portrait of a Nation.* Englewood, Colo.: Westcliffe Publishers, 1992.

Guidoni, Enrico. *Primitive Architecture.* New York: Electa/Rizzoli, 1987.

Hansen, Harry. *Texas: A Guide to the Lone Star State.* American Guide Series. New York: Hastings House, 1969.

Hollon, Eugene W. *The Southwest: Old and New.* Lincoln, Neb., and London: University of Nebraska Press, 1968.

Horgan, Paul. *Great River.* Vols. 1 and 2. Minerva Press, N.Y. 1968.

Hutt, Antony. *North Africa: Islamic Architecture.* London: Scorpion Publications, 1977.

Insight Guides. *Southern Spain.* Hong Kong: APA Publications, 1990.

Iowa, Jerome. *Ageless Adobe.* Santa Fe, N.M.: Sunstone Press, 1985.

James, Harry C. *The Hopi Indians.* Caldwell, Idaho: Caxton Printers, 1956.

Khalili, Nader. *Ceramic Houses.* New York: Harper and Row, 1986.

Kluckhohn, Clyde, and Dorothea Leighton. *The Navaho.* Cambridge, Mass., and London: Harvard University Press, 1974.

Larson, Peggy. *A Sierra Club Naturalist's Guide: The Deserts of the Southwest.* San Francisco: Sierra Club Books, 1977.

Laxalt, Robert. *Nevada.* New York: W. W. Norton, 1977.

Lee, W. Storrs. *California: A Literary Chronicle.* New York: Funk and Wagnalls, 1968.

Lindsay, Lowell and Diana. *The Anza-Borrego Desert Region.* Berkeley, Calif.: Wilderness Press, 1986.

Lipps, Oscar H. *The Little History of the Navajos.* Cedar Rapids, Iowa: Torch Press, 1989.

Lister, Florence C. and Robert H. *Chihuahua: Storehouse of Storms.* Albequerque: University of New Mexico Press, 1966.

———. *Those Who Came Before.* Tucson: University of Arizona Press, 1983.

Look, Al. *1000 Million Years on the Colorado Plateau.* Denver: Bell Publications, 1955.

Nabokov, Peter. *Architecture of Acoma Pueblo: The 1934 Historic American Buildings Survey Project.* Santa Fe, N.M.: Ancient City Press, 1986.

Niehaus, Theodore F. *A Field Guide to Southwestern and Texas Wildflowers.* Peterson Field Guide Series. Boston: Houghton Mifflin, 1984.

Noble, David Grant. *Ancient Ruins of the Southwest.* Flagstaff, Ariz.: Northland Publishing, 1991.

Parkes, Henry Bamford. *A History of Mexico.* Boston: Houghton Mifflin, 1969.

Patch, Edith M., and Carroll Lane Fenton. *Desert Neighbors.* New York: Macmillan, 1940.

Pourade, Richard F. *Anza Conquers the Desert.* San Diego: Copley Press, 1971.

Powell, Major J. W. *The Hopi Villages: The Ancient Province of Tusayan.* Palmer Lake, Calif.: Filter Press, 1972.

Reisner, Marc. *Cadillac Desert.* New York: Viking Penguin, 1986.

Reynolds, Michael E. *Earthship.* Vols. 1 and 2. Taos, N.M.: Solar Survival Press, 1990.

Rolle, Andrew F. *California: A History.* New York: Thomas W. Crowell, 1965.

Sanford, Trenton Ellwood. *The Architecture of the Southwest.* New York: W. W. Norton, 1950.

Scully, Vincent. *Pueblo, Mountain, Village, Dance.* Chicago and London: University of Chicago Press, 1989.

Seth, Sandra and Laurel. *Adobe! Homes and Interiors of Taos, Santa Fe and the Southwest.* Conn.: Architectural Book Publishing, 1988.

Simpson, Ruth DeEtte. *The Hopi Indians.* Los Angeles: Southwest Museum Leaflets, 1971.

Skolle, John. *Azalaii.* New York: Harper and Brothers, 1955.

Southwick, Marcia. *Build with Adobe.* Denver: Sage Books, 1965.

Spicer, Edward H. *Cycles of Conquest.* Tucson: University of Arizona, 1986.

Swift, Jeremy. *The Sahara.* New York: Time-Life Books, 1975.

Titiev, Marshall. *Old Oraibi.* Albuquerque: University of New Mexico Press, 1992.

Trimble, Marshall. *Roadside History of Arizona.* Missoula, Mont.: Mountain Press Publishing, 1986.

Wagoner, Jay J. *Early Arizona, Prehistory to Civil War.* Tucson: University of Arizona Press, 1975.

Waters, Frank. *The Book of Hopi.* New York: Ballantine Books, 1963.

Wharton, Tom and Gayen. *Utah.* Chico, Calif.: Moon Publications, 1991.

White, Owen P. *Texas: An Informal Biography.* New York: G. P. Putnam's Sons, 1945.

Williamson, Ray A. *The Living Sky: The Cosmos of the American Indian.* Norman, Okla., and London: University of Oklahoma Press, 1984.

Woods, Betty. *101 Trips in the Land of Enchantment.* Santa Fe: New Mexico Magazine, 1969.

Writer's Program. *Nevada.* American Guide Series. Portland, Oreg.: Binsfords and Mort, 1957.